OUTSTANDING!

OUTSTANDING!

47 WAYS TO MAKE
YOUR ORGANIZATION
EXCEPTIONAL

JOHN G. MILLER

G. P. Putnam's Sons   New York

PUTNAM

G. P. PUTNAM'S SONS
Publishers Since 1838
Published by the Penguin Group
Penguin Group (USA) Inc., 375 Hudson Street, New York, New York 10014, USA • Penguin
Group (Canada), 90 Eglinton Avenue East, Suite 700, Toronto, Ontario M4P 2Y3, Canada (a division
of Pearson Penguin Canada Inc.) • Penguin Books Ltd, 80 Strand, London WC2R 0RL, England • Penguin
Ireland, 25 St Stephen's Green, Dublin 2, Ireland (a division of Penguin Books Ltd) • Penguin Group (Australia),
250 Camberwell Road, Camberwell, Victoria 3124, Australia • (a division of Pearson Australia Group Pty
Ltd) • Penguin Books India Pvt Ltd, 11 Community Centre, Panchsheel Park, New Delhi–110 017, India •
Penguin Group (NZ), 67 Apollo Drive, Rosedale, North Shore 0632, New Zealand (a division of Pearson
New Zealand Ltd) • Penguin Books (South Africa) (Pty) Ltd, 24 Sturdee Avenue, Rosebank,
Johannesburg 2196, South Africa

Penguin Books Ltd, Registered Offices: 80 Strand, London WC2R 0RL, England

Library of Congress Cataloging-in-Publication Data
Miller, John G.
Outstanding!: 47 ways to make your organization exceptional / John G. Miller.
    p.   cm.
ISBN 978-0-399-15640-3
1. Organizational effectiveness.   2. Organizational change.   3. Customer service.   I. Title.
HD58.9.M554   2010   2009042720
658.4'01—dc22

Printed in the United States of America
1   3   5   7   9   10   8   6   4   2

While the author has made every effort to provide accurate telephone numbers and
Internet addresses at the time of publication, neither the publisher nor the author
assumes any responsibility for errors, or for changes that occur after publication.
Further, the publisher does not have any control over and does not assume any
responsibility for author or third-party websites or their content.

To everyone who cares
enough to improve the place.
You are outstanding!

Contents

Introduction

"Do people fire companies? Yes, they do!"

That was the beginning of an email sent by Steve Chamberlain, an executive with Husqvarna, a global equipment manufacturer, to his team of hundreds. When the email was forwarded to me, those seven words made such an impression that I had to read on.

"I just fired an airline I've flown for years," Steve continued. "Not just because they left me stranded again in Phoenix for the second time in a month but because of the attitude and actions of the employees. Not only did the people on the ground just say, 'Sorry, that's the best we can do' while appearing not to care at all, but the attendants on the plane stood in the galley complaining about their own company and other flight attendants. So I fired them and won't be flying them anymore."

It's amazing how truths sometimes hide right in front of us. I hadn't thought in terms of people firing companies—or any organization—before, but as soon as I read Steve's email, I recognized it happens all the time. I've certainly fired some. I bet you can think of times when you have, too. Steve's note went on with other thoughts specific to his team, but it ended with a crucial question that applies to each and every one of us: "Can any of us afford to be fired by our customers?"

No, we can't. I wrote *Outstanding!* because people fire organizations—but they don't fire the outstanding ones.

Outstanding means being superior, striking, exceptional, clearly noticeable—essentially, to stand out. People are attracted to outstanding organizations. They want to buy from them, sell to them, invest in them, volunteer at them, and work for them. The purpose of this book is to help *every* organization—whether a corporation, nonprofit, small business, government group, church, or charity—work to be one of those organizations. *Outstanding!* is a distillation of the essential things we need to be thinking and doing—or, in some cases, *not* thinking and doing—in order to help our organizations stand out from the rest. These are the absolute best ideas and practices I've come across working with hundreds of organizations of all kinds since 1986, when I began my sales career in the field of training and organizational development. Each chapter presents one concept, with no ranking implied. That is, #47 is no less important than #1, and #16 is no more so than #26. Each one stands on its own and is equally worthy of our attention. But *you* will ultimately decide which of the 47 is critical to your organization right now. Some will inspire you, some will challenge you, and some will do both. You may disagree with some or think they are not relevant to your organization—and that's fine, too. As long as an idea challenges our current thinking and practices, it's worthwhile. But my expectation is that for the vast majority of these ideas you'll nod your head while reading and think, *Yes, that makes sense. We need to do that.* And then, when you reread and reexplore this book (since repetition is the motor of learning), different "ways" will become more meaningful at different times.

I should also say what this book is *not* about. It's not about technology and systems. It's not about legal strategies and compliance with government regulations. It's not about the latest and greatest ideas—or fads—streaming from business schools or cable television "gurus." We won't be covering anything about branding or how to perform an effective new product launch. And there will be few, if any, trendy buzzwords in this book—I assure you. What I do promise is practical, commonsense ideas that work. When it comes to good ideas, there is no "sell by" date. The word "timeless" comes to mind.

Outstanding! is for *anyone* who cares about "improving the place"—from executives to middle managers to team leaders to frontline staff. And keep in mind that teams, departments, branch offices, districts, and divisions are organizations, too. Don't sit back waiting for people above or below you to get started. Strengthening even one corner of an organization is better than doing nothing at all. Organizations are made up of individuals, and outstanding organizations are created by individuals doing outstanding things. It will be up to you—and others in your organization—to make it happen.

In the end, *Outstanding!* will show each of us 47 ways to help our organization reach levels of performance and reputation that few achieve. My hope is that *Outstanding!* will move you—no matter your title or position—to cause your organization to become the best it can be. In other words, to help it be *outstanding*! It's an exciting vision, so let's get started right now. Enjoy!

CHAPTER ONE

Be Fast

While ordering lunch at a fast-food place (on this particular day, it was a Wendy's), I noticed a digital clock on the wall where they were handling drive-through customers. In big red numbers, it would start at zero, tick up in time by seconds, and then suddenly reset back to zero and start counting up again. I asked the woman taking my money what the clock was for, and she said, "That shows us how quickly we're handling the customers outside." *Interesting,* I thought. So I continued, "And what do you do with the information? Do you look at your average serve time daily?" And right then, her supervisor, listening to our conversation, jumped in enthusiastically and answered my question; "Oh, no, we check our score every three hours. We need to be fast, you know!" And I thought, *Don't we all.*

How fast is your organization?

Outstanding organizations have a tremendous sense of urgency. People get things done—quickly. There is little waiting around for approval, there are few meetings, and even fewer "committee decisions." They resist creating burdensome policies, and where policies do become roadblocks, managers carry a sharp pair of scissors, constantly clearing the way for their people by cutting the red tape.

An executive at H. B. Fuller, an esteemed organization founded in 1887 in St. Paul, Minnesota, once shared with me this colorful metaphor: "John, it's a bad day for us when a snake slithers into the lobby and we all encircle the reptile to assess the situation, discuss where it came from, who let it in, and what species it is. It's a good day when someone just grabs a shovel and cuts its head off." Apologies to snake lovers—of which I'm one—but what he was saying is true. When the bullets are flying, don't call a meeting. Don't stand around and contemplate. Do something!

The fact is, some decisions simply do not need to be a big deal. If there's a snake in the lobby, take care of it. If you're looking for a vendor to help on a project, find some candidates, check them out, and pick one. Way too often the many hoops organizations make their people jump through, plus the number of people invited into the decision-making process, cause decisions that should realistically take a day or a week to drag on for months, sometimes years.

What ineffective organizations don't understand is how much money is pouring out the back door due to these sorts of things. Not only does it cost the time and energy—and compensation—of everyone involved, but every minute spent on one thing is a minute not available to work on something else. I have honestly seen "buying committees" spend, say, $250,000 in collective salary cost to make a $50,000 decision. I bet you've seen this happen, too. It's math that just doesn't add up. One manager at a Fortune 500 firm shared candidly, "I do not work for an out-standing organization. We are a good organization with a good reputation, but decisions take too long. Our market moves at lightning speed, and it seems we're always a step or two behind while some un-known, unnamed committee meets to plan their next meeting. We've lost multimillion-dollar contracts while waiting and waiting and waiting for decisions to be reached."

To be fast does not mean we should be foolish

and be in such a rush that we make mistakes. Taking the time to make good decisions is critical—but outstanding organizations make good decisions *faster*. And they do it by creating a culture that sends the message: Let's get it done . . . yesterday!

In a way, we're all like the staff at Wendy's, with a clock on the wall, ticking away precious time. Let's make the best use of every second.

Be fast!

CHAPTER TWO

Be Humble

When I left the training firm I sold for after a decade of calling on senior managers, I *really* wanted to author a book titled *The Arrogance of Management*. But, alas, I didn't think executives would buy it.

Ben Franklin said this about pride: "Even if I could conceive that I had completely overcome it, I would probably be proud of my humility." That tongue-in-cheek humor really states a truth: After making the big sale, delivering the project on time, launching a winning product, or landing a promotion, it can be seriously hard to show humility. Yet that's what we find in outstanding organizations.

Sheryll, a project coordinator in information services with a major healthcare organization, told me, "Our CIO sent an amazing message to all the employees in our department. It makes me want to give him a big hug! But since it's probably not appropriate to do that, I am just going to stop by his office to thank him for being a marvelous role model, and let him know how much I appreciate his accountable actions!"

She went on to tell me about an incident that seemed minor initially, but snowballed into a problem for this executive. To save money, he had decided to change cake vendors. Yes, you read that right: *cake*. His technology team has a long-standing and highly valued "Cake Day" tradition in which they recognize service anniversaries, birthdays, and other such milestones by getting cake for everyone to share, and the CIO had made the decision to switch to a cheaper cake supplier. Naturally, these celebrations are important to the hundreds of people in the department, but the CIO didn't understand how important they were—and that's fair. Often in life one person doesn't know what something means to another. However, on top of making the change to a possibly less tasty product, his email to everyone announcing the switch also facetiously described the change as a "drastic cost-cutting measure." Though there was absolutely no bad intent on his part, the proverbial molehill grew into the mountain, and in came feedback indicating that he now had a mini-crisis on his hands.

So he handled it with grace and aplomb, taking a rare action by those "at the top": *He apologized.* In a broadcast email, he wrote contritely that he shouldn't have made light of this change and that he owed them a sincere apology. He accepted responsibility for the mess and even claimed poor judgment. He went on to confess that he doesn't always choose the right words, but assured everyone that his colleagues mean the world to him and are his highest priority.

Rarely have I come across such a powerful example of being humble. I believe that humility is the cornerstone of leadership. Others do, too. Russ Gasdia, vice president of sales and marketing for Purdue Pharma, sums it up well. When asked to list three characteristics of an "effective leader," he said, "Humility, humility, and humility. They know they make mistakes, accept feedback from others in order to learn, admit they don't always know what's right, and recognize it's not 'all about them.' When they succeed, they are humble. When they fail, they are humble. And lastly, they *never* think they are more important than the customer!"

Humility is a key trait of outstanding organizations—and of individuals. Humility helps people be more likable and approachable, work better with others, and give better service to customers. It enables departments and teams to collaborate with other departments and teams. Perhaps most important, it allows people to communicate more freely, creating a culture of authenticity and accountability that every outstanding organization requires. Beyond all this, it might even win us a hug or two—and maybe there's nothing wrong with that!

CHAPTER THREE

Keep the Mission "Top of Mind"

I took my son, Michael, at age eight, to a youth wrestling program. As local college stars demonstrated complicated wrestling holds and maneuvers, I noticed Mike and his mat partner getting confused and frustrated. They just didn't get it and Mike started to cry. I called him over and said, "Mike, let's head on home, okay?" He was most agreeable. As we hopped into the car, still baffled over why the coaches had taught sophisticated moves to such young children, I grabbed my cell and called my dad, E. J. "Jimmy" Miller, Jr., who was Cornell University's wrestling coach for more than twenty-five years. "Dad," I asked, "if you were going to instruct eight-year-old boys in wrestling, what's the first thing you'd teach them?" Without a second's hesitation he replied, "I'd teach them the purpose of the sport, son." *Sounds good,* I thought. He went on to explain, "I would help them know before learning anything else that the purpose of wrestling is to put the other man on his back."

"That's great, Pop," I said. "What would you teach next?" He smiled through the phone, saying, "I would then teach them to stay off their own back!"

Purpose comes first. What a great lesson for all of us. Much has been said about the importance of purpose in people's lives, but it's every bit as important for an organization. That's why it's so surprising to see what a lousy job some organizations still do in this arena. I've interacted with too many frontline people on the phone who, first, could not give me directions to the company's building and, second, were unable to answer the question "What does your organization do?" If they couldn't answer those basic questions, what are the odds they would've known why the organization existed?

While checking out at our favorite grocery store, I was caught off guard when the cashier asked me what I thought was a random question: "Stamps or ice today, sir?" I looked at her quizzically and responded, "Stamps or ice? With thousands of items in this store, why do you ask me if I want stamps or ice?" She lowered her voice, leaned toward me a bit, and said, "Because if I don't ask I get written up." Now that's purpose!

What too many managers don't understand is that people will do practically anything (as long as it's legal and ethical) if they understand *why* they are doing it—and they'll do it joyfully, with their full heart. The truth is this: *purpose powers passion*. The organization's mission can excite people, giving them fuel, if you will, to do their jobs each day. It helps them feel like they are part of something larger than themselves, and wards off the "I owe, I owe, so off to work I go!" mentality which, sadly, is all too common.

For some organizations there is no doubt about why they exist. It's as if the word "mission" is built right into their name. Of course, for the Denver Rescue Mission—founded in 1892 in Denver, Colorado—it is. In his own words, Brad Meuli, a longtime banking executive and now CEO of this venerable institution, shared these thoughts:

Employed by a faith-based non-profit, our people really believe what they do is important, that it matters for eternity, and that they are called to be here. This heart for serving and powerful desire to help others is at the core of who we are. How terrific it is to work for an organization where the staff not only believe in but truly live each day the commandment to "love your neighbor as yourself." Our team of more than 150 gets up in the morning wanting to come to work! How else would it be possible to serve 800 homeless people on any given day? How else would it be possible to serve 700,000 meals annually? How else would it be possible to love, encourage, and work with people who have alienated everyone in those lives because of substance abuse, and then see their lives changed to that of productive, self-sufficient citizens free from addiction? This would not be possible if our staff was not deeply committed to believing that people matter. This is why we exist.

For every organization the *why* is what it's all about. If a receptionist can't tell a caller or visitor what the organization does and why it does it, that's a problem. If the supermarket cashier pushes products out of fear rather than a desire to serve, that's a problem. We need to infuse our mission into everything we do—and doing so is not a one-time job. While visiting with Martin Bischoff, vice chairman of Citizens Bank based in Rhode Island, he said, "We must communicate more than what to do and how to do it; we've got to tell people the 'why' over and over and over again. It never ends."

Martin couldn't be more right. But this is not only the job of the vice chairmen of the world. People at all levels are accountable for knowing the mission, talking it up, and making it the impetus for their daily work. It's everyone's responsibility to be able to answer the critical question "Why do we exist?"

In an outstanding organization, the mission is always top of mind.

Chapter Four

Get Actions in Line with Values

Nowadays, we hear a lot of talk about "alignment," and I suspect it means different things to different people. To me, it's all about getting the values—sometimes called "guiding principles"—that are espoused by the organization in sync with the actions of its people. Some organizations do this well, and some don't.

I entered a coffee and bagel shop one morning and ordered a salt bagel with cream cheese. As an afterthought, I added, "Oh, may I have my bagel toasted, please?" Without looking up, the person helping me said, "We don't toast bagels." More out of curiosity than anything else, I said, "I'd think a lot of people would like their bagels toasted in the morning." At that, he stopped his work mid-slice, looked at me, and said, "Sir, if I toasted *your* bagel, I'd have *everybody* in here wanting toasted bagels!" This made me wonder, *Hmm, would it be so bad to have customers lined up out the door and down the block ready to trade their hard-earned cash for a toasted bagel? I think not!*

Now, I bet the story behind the story is the executives of this company at some point held a mountain-top retreat to ponder key questions such as "How do we increase traffic to our stores?" and "What can we do to raise our customer satisfaction scores?" Good questions, and from my experience, I suspect they concluded that they should establish an organizational value like, *IT'S ALL ABOUT THE CUSTOMER!* Then, returning to their offices, they slapped the new phrase on the wall, posted it on their website, and printed it on little plastic laminated wallet cards. *There,* the senior management team thought, *we're on the right track now!* But the reality is this: The non-bagel-toasting employee in the field essentially told a customer with a special request the exact opposite.

Obviously, the problem with this picture is the declared values of the organization and the behavior on the front line are not aligned. And getting them aligned is no easy thing; it takes hard work. But when we do create that much-sought-after alignment, we are well rewarded.

Debbie Slocum, head of human resources for Husqvarna Construction Products, like many people today, customizes her email signature with something important to her: Husqvarna's "global core values." Here's how it appears on her emails:

Customers First * Professionalism * Teamwork
Always with passion and a sense of urgency!

Though the message in these words is excellent, the real value to the customer comes from the great job Husqvarna has done in getting their stated values in sync with actions at the grassroots—where the real work gets done. But don't take it from me. The evidence is in this note from Chuck Gallagher, a branch manager for United Rentals and a Husqvarna customer:

My commercial contractor client, JE Dunn, called late on a Friday to rent a Husqvarna industrial saw, but we didn't have any in stock. When I called Husqvarna to set up a pickup for JE Dunn, I learned that the Husqvarna distribution center was closing for the day—and week. Fortunately, Michelle had answered. After listening to my problem, she asked, "Where does the saw need to go?" I told her the location of JE Dunn's construction site, and she responded, "Well, I could take it to them."

"Um, okay."

So, late on a Friday, Michelle went out of her way to deliver a big saw to my client. The value to JE Dunn was keeping their crew working all weekend. And it was all possible because Michelle put a customer first, instead of saying, "Sorry, we're closing." When I spoke to JE Dunn, they were extremely impressed. Michelle sure made us look good! Thanks to her, United Rentals ordered two more Husqvarna saws so we'll have plenty in stock to rent to our customers!

On the surface, Chuck's story is one of outstanding customer service by Michelle. On a deeper level, it's a perfect picture of the alignment so many organizations strive for and never achieve. Alignment comes from believing that the values of the organization are important, and then practicing those values—even when it's not convenient. Any organization can espouse great-sounding values, but if they aren't translated into action they are nothing more than slogans. Alignment is a powerful force for making any organization outstanding.

CHAPTER FIVE

See Everyone as a Customer

Are you familiar with the concept of "360-degree feedback"? Sometimes it's called "multi-rater feedback." The idea is that lots of people, such as your peers, your boss—and if you manage others, your staff—all give input on how you're doing. The rationale for this is sound: These people know you, they see you in action, and they have an opinion about your performance. It's a valuable, if not sometimes painful, process. Everyone gets a chance to have their say . . . about you! And, why shouldn't they? After all, *they* are your customers.

In most organizations, we've learned that we have two kinds of customers. We've gone through the workshops where we've gotten out the flip charts and divided people into two groups under these headings: External and Internal. External customers are those people who buy and consume our products and services. Internal customers are the people who work for our organization. The lesson is that serving our internal customers is every bit as important to our success as serving our external ones. The idea is not all that new, and I suspect many organizations have incorporated both the lesson and the language into their culture. I mention it because I think we can do this in a cleaner, simpler, more effective way. Let's put the flip charts away, drop the labels we've created, and change the definition of a customer, using the 360-Degree Customer Concept: A customer is *anyone* who has a legitimate expectation of me.

So, a customer, viewed in this light, would be our boss, peers, staff, other departments, the home office, and so on—as well as any "outsider" who buys from, sells to, volunteers at, attends, or donates to our organization. Truly, anyone we might be in a position to serve on any day in any capacity—360 degrees around us.

Viewing everyone as a customer can be truly enlightening. The day after a speaking engagement where I shared this idea, I received an email from a manager. He wrote: "Using the 360-Degree Customer Concept, I see the world with new eyes today. No longer do I see 'my people' but customers all around me here at work! Because of my new view, I will be a better manager and coach." Actually, he just might now be an outstanding one.

There are other people, though, who struggle with this concept. They ask: "Well, who defines 'legitimate'?" Or they declare, "I can accept it for the field salespeople but not for the IT department!" But it's not called the *192*-Degree Customer Concept or the *287*-Degree Customer Concept. It's the *360*-Degree Customer Concept, and it means dropping the artificial categories and labels we've conjured up and serving people *all around us.*

The beauty of the idea is in its simplicity, as well as reinforcing the underlying principle and truth that we exist to serve. Who is a customer? Everyone. Who do I serve? Everybody. The message is clear, inspiring, and foolproof. It also helps us be outstanding. Most organizations are committed to service and many have embraced the idea of "internal" customers. So in order to stand out from the rest, we need to take our commitment to service higher and higher. The 360-Degree Customer Concept is a practical tool that helps us get there.

CHAPTER SIX

Fight the Fat—In Good Times or Bad

In 1988, I had the honor of lunching with Marvin Schwan of Schwan's Sales Enterprises, Inc. Schwan's is a multibillion-dollar, route-delivery food company that was originally founded by Marvin's dad as a dairy in the 1940s. I was a thirty-year-old sales guy at the time, selling leadership and sales training programs in the Minneapolis/St. Paul area. The day of our meeting, I made the drive out to the farm country of southwestern Minnesota, where the corn grows tall and the mosquitoes even taller. As we ate in a small-town diner, this soft-spoken billionaire told me something I'd never heard before—and never forgot: "John, sales cover sins. And *lots* of sales cover *lots* of sins."

I probably didn't quite get it then, but I think I do

now. The "sins" organizations commit are things like not paying attention to costs, taking clients for granted, ignoring market trends, failing to improve inefficient systems, disregarding customer input, not worrying about the competition, and so on. And Marvin's comment meant that when dollars rush in like a dyke upstream has burst, it's easy to look past those sins. In other words, when times are good, we let our standards slip. We relax and stop doing the things we know we could—and should. The things that make our organizations outstanding.

I once asked personal finance author and radio host Dave Ramsey what *one* message he'd share with individuals about their money. He said, "John, I would tell them to *bother*. Bother to pay attention. Bother to be intentional with their money. Money leaves those who don't pay attention. Successful people concentrate; they pay attention to their finances. Said differently, they *bother*."

Dave's advice applies equally well to organizations. If we all bothered to run our organizations every single day as if times were tough, fighting the fat by keeping the sins of waste and inefficiency to a minimum, we'd be much better prepared to weather the inevitable economic downturns that come. We'd also keep the focus we need to be an outstanding organization.

Chatting with Craig Beck, a school superintendent, he shared that when he got the job he targeted fifty-three positions for elimination. Not people, not personalities, but positions. Simply put, the district had gotten fat. During our conversation, he chuckled, saying, "Yeah, I wasn't all that popular around here!" I responded with, "Well, I bet some people thought it was a good thing to do." He then said, "Actually, the truth is, I got more calls and emails from staff saying 'thank you' than I could count! It did make us a better organization."

It's really true: When we bother to bother, it makes us better all around.

CHAPTER SEVEN

Give People Tools, Not Slogans

"Think outside the box!"

"Winners never quit and quitters never win!"

"Attitude is everything!"

"Be a team!"

"Dare to achieve!"

"Just do it!"

Slap statements like these on the hallways inside your building, and on the walls of people's minds, and what will you get? Nothing, or at least nothing of lasting value. Slogans may sound great, but in order to take the organization to higher levels, people don't need platitudes—they need tools.

Say I'm a lumberjack working in the forest and you're my manager. Every day I work hard, chopping down trees with my trusty, double-bladed ax, which I keep sharp enough to split a hair. You come out to see me for my performance review and inform me that even though I just finished a record year, I need to produce at a rate of 20 percent above my previous level. In other words, management is "raising the bar." I'm amazed at this news, and stare at you as if either I didn't hear you correctly or you're one limb short of a tree. "But, boss," I cry, "I'm working twelve hours a day now! I only take a break to sharpen my ax and I always skip lunch. How in the world can I produce more?" As I'm pleading for you to understand, you walk away, leaving me thinking, *Uh-oh. I said too much!* Then, you return with a brand-new, shiny chainsaw, well-oiled, gassed up, and ready to go. "Is that for me?" I ask, hopefully.

"She's all yours! Isn't she a beaut?"

"Terrific, boss! Thanks! And oh, by the way, you wanted twenty percent? I'll give you thirty!"

In my book *QBQ! The Question Behind the Question*, I suggest that people shouldn't waste time asking questions like, "When are we going to get more tools?" but instead ask, "What can I do to succeed with the resources I have?" I firmly believe that's the best path for an individual in any role or position, but the suggestion isn't meant to let management off the hook. In fact, it's quite the opposite. Yes, individuals need to do their best with the resources provided, but it's equally important for organizations to give people the tools they need to succeed, and here's why: When people are faced with a task to complete, a goal to achieve, or a hill to climb, they ask themselves critical questions, like, *Can I do it?* and *Am I able?* People must be able to answer those questions with a resounding *Yes!* if they are to get the job done, and having the right tools gives them that confidence.

We intuitively know that people need to believe they can do the job. The problem is, it's tempting to try to raise people's performance through slogans, platitudes, and inspiration alone. Certainly, a lively motivational message can be fun to hear, but when we hold the January "Hype Me Up High" meetings where mountain climbers are invited to speak because, well, they climbed a mountain, we give people very little. Yes, the speaker will awe us with the dangers they faced and the glory they found, and show us the PowerPoint presentation of icicles hanging from parkas and chins. We'll shake their hand, buy their book, and get their autograph. It'll be a great time! However, no matter what people hear in a motivational meeting, whether in the grand ballroom of a warm-weather resort or one-on-one in the boss's office, they walk right out and into "The Wall of Reality"— defined as a big stack of work and ever-increasing expectations. If we have not given them anything practical that they can use, we've failed them.

People need more. Only when we provide them with the right tools will they be able to confidently say, "You wanted twenty percent? I'll give you thirty!" Let's give people the tools they need.

CHAPTER EIGHT

Make Meetings Meaningful

One of my daughters, just a month after entering the workforce after college, said, "Dad, I'm not getting anything done on the job and feel like I am slipping behind—and I just started." When I asked what was happening, she vented, "I'm spending half of my time in meetings that are absolutely worthless!" And I thought, *Huh. With all the books and training on the market on how to run an effective meeting—this is* still *happening?* But apparently it is, and not just in my daughter's organization. I recently asked a new contact at a client firm what his position was and he said, "I am a PMA."

"What exactly is that?" I asked.

"Professional Meeting Attender."

The truth is, people do need face-to-face time to accomplish certain things, but we sometimes forget that most real work is done *outside* the conference room. Outstanding organizations simply don't waste people's precious time in meaningless meetings. Someone once said the worst of all murders is the killing of time. Bad meetings certainly can do that, plus be the death of enthusiasm, innovation, morale, and productivity. So here are some practical ideas for how to make meetings more productive:

> **Have a clear leader:** Only one person can run a meeting. Any more than that creates confusion and inaction, which are exactly what you *don't* want in a meeting.
>
> **Use a list:** Some say you should set an agenda, laying out what you'll talk about and in what order, but agendas can actually be confining and hurt creativity. The more meaningful way to go is for the meeting leader to create a list of whatever items need to be covered and share the list with the attendees before the meeting begins—and then do your dead-level best to stick to it.
>
> **Keep the list small:** Trying to cover too many things in one meeting leads to skimming topics and creates no real value for the organization. Keep the number down and people will leave

meetings feeling energized rather than over-whelmed and exhausted.

Focus on the right things: Spending time at-tempting to hash out things people have no control over gets nothing accomplished and only makes people feel frustrated and nega-tive. Stay focused on the things you can actu-ally do something about. And remember this: Don't even hold the meeting if there are no problems to solve or decisions to be made.

Meet at the right time: The wrong times for a meeting are typically right before and after lunch, at the end of the day, early Monday morn-ing, and late on Friday. You know your culture. Work to find a time when people are up for the meeting.

Consider the meeting space: Dull rooms, bad chairs, and the "same old, same old" location can lead to stale meetings. Freshen the space up, if need be. Change it up, too, from time to time. No need to meet in the same place every time. "Variety is the spice of life," as the saying goes. It also makes for more meaningful meetings.

Invite the right people: Look at the invitee list and if someone's presence isn't critical—or if their need to be there is minimal—delete their name and let them remain at their work area to get some real work done.

Prepare: People coming unprepared drains energy, wastes time, and causes the group to get little done. But also make sure there is something to prepare for. As one teacher in a Texas school district told me: "We have way too many faculty meetings that could've been summed up in an email."

Be punctual: Starting late (and running long) is insidious: Over time, people think, *Why be on time? We never start on time.* And it just gets worse and worse. I know that stuff can happen to delay a meeting or cause it to go beyond the stated ending time, but to the extent you can, get back on schedule. And if you're done early, for heaven's sake—get out!

Control tangents: The person running the meeting must be willing to terminate digressions. As one meeting "prisoner" told me, "If the leader isn't strong, tangents reign. It is *so* irritating to sit there while someone goes off about something that has nothing to do with why we got together." Another said, "It's so awkward when they ramble on and on. I just want to scream 'STOP TALKING!'" When the conversation gets off track, it's the leader's job to pull it back. It's best to do it in a firm but nonconfrontational way. But in the end, we need to be less concerned with hurt feelings and more concerned with being productive.

If someone's done, let them leave: If a person's "topic" has been covered, please release them. Staying the full length of the meeting after a person's topic has been covered is a waste.

Stay standing: This is a radical idea for most organizations, but Sentara Healthcare of Virginia, operating more than one hundred care-giving sites, including seven acute care hospitals, holds "huddles" every morning with the explicit purpose of exchanging critical info and solving problems. (What else is a meeting for?) These "no-chair" gatherings, which I have attended, are crisp, precise, and, dare I say, outstanding.

Outstanding organizations make the best use of a most precious resource: time. Let's get in, get out, and get back to work!

CHAPTER NINE

Speak Up!

If being *outstanding* means to stand *out*, might it also mean to stand *up* and *speak* up?

At the end of a long strategy-setting meeting, the boss asks the team, "So, do we all agree with this new plan?" Heads nod, thumbs go up, and polite smiles shine. *Great,* the boss thinks, *we're all on the same page.* Yet not three minutes later, at a Water Cooler Huddle, people speak in hushed voices: "Wow. That was a dumb idea!" "Where does he come up with these schemes?" or "Doesn't she know it'll never work?!" And then, even worse, people blame: "Well, they don't allow us to speak up" or "My boss doesn't really want input from me."

What's wrong with this picture? If people don't agree, why didn't they say so in the meeting? I can tell you from conversations I've had, this is an ongoing frustration for countless executives and managers.

In my experience, the main reason why people don't speak up is a very human thing: We're enslaved to the opinions of others. Other people's opinions can at times be so important to us that they literally shape what we say and do—or don't say and do. Our all-too-common need for approval can easily become the tie that binds, and it takes strength and courage to break free from that and say what we really think. But for the good of both the organization and ourselves, it's imperative that we do it. We need to speak up.

Now, I don't mean we should give unlimited rein to anything and everything that is on our minds. It's not advisable to approach a colleague with something like, "It's really looking like the years are catching up with you!" or to ask your boss, "When did you buy that outfit—the eighties?" But we can sure do better in this area, and it starts with the way we think. Great organizations believe and commit to this: *We will not have any "elephants in the room" at our place.*

In some organizations, there's a strong "parent-child syndrome" that inhibits people from speaking up. Anyone with a bigger and longer title is a "mom" or a "dad" and everyone else is a "child." I'm not saying we *are* children, just that there's a similar dynamic in play: The "children" see the "parents" as powerful beings that have the ability to grant or deny favor, so they are afraid to disagree, object, and speak up too boldly and bluntly. More generally, this is a fear of authority, and it's a problem I've seen over and over again.

An organization simply cannot be exceptional if people don't speak up and candidly share what they see, think, and believe. Otherwise, ideas are left inside people's minds instead of out on the table, available for dissection and exploration. Creative problem-solving suffers, as do morale, teamwork, and good old esprit de corps. Even our energy and enthusiasm are dampened. It's just not healthy for individuals or organizations when people don't openly share their ideas, observations, and concerns.

Nicholas Murray Butler, an American philosopher, said, "Necessity does the work of courage." Without question, having people at every level speak up is a necessity for an outstanding organization. We need a culture that supports that. And I mean *really* supports it, not just gives it lip service. I've facilitated many a session where the boss says, "Now, today we're taking off the stripes. No titles! We're equals in this room." But people know from experience that when the meeting ends, the stripes will go right back on, so they'd better watch what they say. We can do better than that—and we must.

Let's create an environment that not only gives people permission to speak up, but encourages it, even requires it—and makes it safe to do so. But ultimately, it's up to each of us as individuals to stand up and share what's on our mind. For that, let's look to ourselves and continually work to develop the courage necessary to do so. It's not always easy, but it's better for the organization—and for each of us.

Speak up!

CHAPTER TEN

Set the Cultural Tone

David Levin, my friend and colleague for many years, conducted a training workshop for Philips Lifeline, a small firm that had been recently acquired by the major corporation Philips. Post session, he and Jami Ritter, senior director at Philips Lifeline, chatted about her organization's culture, and she mentioned that she loved working there. David responded with how impressed he was with the people he'd met—how friendly, warm, and outgoing everyone was. Jami agreed, and said it was a refreshing change from the culture of a larger company for which she'd worked previously.

"What do you suppose makes the difference?" David asked. "Is it just that this is a smaller organization?" "Oh, no," she replied. "It's Ron. Our CEO, Ron Feinstein, who just retired after seventeen years. All those traits you mentioned—they describe Ron perfectly. That's just who he is."

I imagine we've all heard that "culture starts at the top," and it's even possible that you're tired of hearing it, but setting the tone for an organization's culture *is* a duty that comes with being in an influential position. Sometimes that duty is fulfilled through behaviors and persona, like Ron. At other times, it's simply a well-timed, pithy comment that serves as a powerful reminder of the culture we want or already have and desire to maintain.

I spoke at a leadership conference consisting of principals and staff of Cumberland County Schools in Fayetteville, North Carolina. Afterward, Superintendent Dr. Bill Harrison and his direct reports, about a half-dozen folks, kindly took me to lunch. Once we'd ordered, the conversation really took off, soon reaching a dull roar. This team that leads more than six thousand staff and fifty-four thousand students began sharing about the complexity of public education, the communication problems they face, the barrage of changes hitting them, and all the "stuff" they face each day. *The parents! The kids! Tight budgets! Testing! Government standards! Technology!* As the din grew, I noticed that Dr. Bill was observing his team with a twinkle in his eye. Finally, he spoke. "Ah, but let's all remember: No excuses." All chatter ceased. Quiet enveloped the group and everyone nodded. Dr. Bill's comment did not put his team on the spot or shame them, it simply reminded them of a core value—personal responsibility—in which the Cumberland County team wholeheartedly believes but had, just for a moment, forgotten.

Straying from our ideals, our stated values, happens to all of us from time to time, but when Dr. Bill performed a simple "reset" with his fine team, all was well again.

Of course, it's not just about CEOs and school district superintendents. Jami, the senior director, sets the tone for her department, as do managers for their staff, and supervisors and team leaders for the front line. Individuals who manage nobody but themselves even have a hand in all this, too. And the same idea applies outside of work as well. Boy and Girl Scout leaders set the tone for the troop, a pastor for his church, a sports coach for her team, a sergeant for his platoon, a teacher for the classroom, and a parent in the home. When it comes to setting the cultural tone in outstanding organizations, it's everyone's job.

Eastview High School in Apple Valley, Minnesota,

really gets this. In the words of assistant principal Rob Franchino, "We have created a unique culture here regarding high expectations and the guiding principles that are designed to become a way of life. One of them is personal accountability, and we underscore that value in a visible way: On our outside doors are stenciled the words 'It Starts with Me!' So students and staff see this message when they come into the school every day."

Rob understands how critical it is to define the culture clearly and that it's everyone's responsibility, even his own. He went on to say, "I know it's *my* job to weave the right ideals and behaviors into *my* life each day." He couldn't be more on target: Setting the cultural tone "starts with me."

Why does this culture thing matter? To begin with, certain cultures attract certain kinds of people, and we need to recruit—and keep—the people we want and need. Outstanding organizations need outstanding team members, and the tone of an organization plays a huge role in who comes on board and who stays on board. Additionally, the cultural tone has an impact on how problems get solved, the way people speak to one another, the levels of innovation and creativity, the trust between employees and management, and the risks individuals are willing to take—not to mention the "fun factor" of working there. The culture even affects how the phone is answered, and that's critical since there's no second chance to make a first impression with that all-important customer. In the end, setting the right cultural tone is everything—and everyone's involved.

CHAPTER ELEVEN

Don't Speak in Code

Though I have worked with a wide variety of organizations for years, I do not always understand what people are saying to me. I actually sometimes wonder if it's me. Chatting with Ned, a sales vice president, he said, "I had a guy on my team as a regional manager and it wasn't going well, so I helped him separate." *Separate?* I just did the blank stare thing until understanding finally came to me, and I said, "Oh, he doesn't work here anymore." That's not as bad as some. The term "downsizing," for example, and, even worse, "right-sizing" seem especially grating when what's really going on is that we're cutting jobs and letting people go.

Certainly, we need to choose our words carefully because words do matter. And some will argue that putting a positive spin on uncomfortable truths can have positive benefits, which may be true in some cases. But when we start talking in such a way that what we say no longer makes sense to those who don't understand the "code," we have done everyone a disservice.

Speaking in code manifests itself in many ways. When I speak to a group, I have fun—and the audience does, too—making light of some of the language that has cropped up in our organizations. When I say, tongue in cheek, "Now, I am sure in your organization you don't have any problems . . . [long pause] . . . but I bet you have plenty of 'opportunities,'" the laughter rolls around the room because they recognize the reality that we too often replace words like "problem" with heavily coded ones such as "opportunity," "challenge," "issue," and "situation."

There are dangers when people don't speak plainly, especially when there are real problems to face. When an executive gets up at a meeting and talks about the "great opportunity ahead" rather than speaking transparently about the fact that sales are off, morale is down, market share has eroded, and profits are being squeezed, the lack of authenticity eats away at the trust employees have in their organization. It can send the message that it's more important to *look* good than *be* good. Appearances and facades have now won out over reality.

On a more practical level, when a manager speaks in code during a performance review, giving an employee vague feedback about the person's "opportunities" rather than being specific about areas to improve or (heavens!) weaknesses, it robs the individual of the chance to grow. How can someone remove a weakness they don't know about? It also robs the organization of the chance to have a more highly trained person.

There are many reasons we speak in code. One is our fear of offending people (a favorite T-shirt I've seen says, "I'm offended that you're offended!"). Another is that we get caught up using the trendy "buzz" words of the day. While on a tour at a client site, I noticed lots of empty cubicles. When I asked where everyone was, I was told, "They are fulfilling their social responsibility today." I politely requested a translation and received this response: "Our people are out painting park benches and picking up roadside trash to help the community." *Oh,* I thought, *I really need to get out more.*

Furthermore, some think speaking plainly and directly makes them sound less intelligent. But in my humble opinion, I think it's better to be clear and understood than to sound super smart. Last, there is the very real embarrassment factor. Someone once said that all lies are designed to protect the one not telling the truth; a device to guard humans from emotional pain. For example, when a public official struggles to apologize for an ill-advised comment, rather than instinctively using the two and a half magic words "I'm sorry!" out pops self-protecting code-speak such as, "I could have calibrated those words differently." Huh? Much better would be an old-fashioned, from-the-heart apology.

They say that truth is like surgery, it hurts but it heals. Let's speak truthfully and plainly in our organizations rather than in code.

CHAPTER TWELVE

Value Ideas over Politics

One of my favorite television commercials is a FedEx ad in which several people are sitting around a conference table in what looks to be a typical corporate meeting. The conversation goes like this:

> Gray-haired Senior Executive: "We have got to cut costs, people! Ideas?"
>
> Junior Guy: "We could open an account on FedEx.com and save ten percent on online express shipping."
>
> (Long pause, while Junior Guy is completely ignored.)
>
> Gray-haired Senior Executive: "Okay, how 'bout this: We open an account on FedEx.com and we save ten percent on online express shipping?!"

People around the table: "Brilliant!" "That is
wonderful!" "Great idea!" "Right on the
nose!" "Yeah, that's good."

It's certainly a funny commercial, but *why* is it so
funny? Because the scene around the table is so real.
In fact, it hits so close to home, it raises serious concerns for our organizations. An organization's success depends not only on its people, but also on the
quality of its ideas. How do we outsmart our competition? How do we streamline, grow, and achieve our
goals? How do we win?

Ideas!

We can't afford to overlook or dismiss an idea just
because it didn't come from the "right" person.

The essence of organizational politics is when
who said something is more important than *what was
said*. That is, the source of an idea ranks higher than
the merit of the idea itself. That's the mind-set this ad
ridicules, and this sort of political thinking does
nothing but harm to an organization. The question
should never be "Who said it?" but only "Will it help
us succeed?"

Let's leave politics to politicians. Inside our organizations, it's better to create cultures that encour-

age input and sharing, where we benefit from the experience and wisdom of all people. When ideas come, make sure to use the best ones, no matter where they're from—because *ideas* are the lifeblood of all exceptional organizations.

CHAPTER THIRTEEN

Forgive Mistakes

About to head home after running errands, I hopped into my pickup truck (required transportation in Colorado), buckled up, and prepared to back out of my parking spot. I looked to my right and noticed a young mom lifting a toddler out of her minivan, which was parked next to me. Focusing on them, I failed to look directly behind me as I backed up. Suddenly, I heard a loud crunch of metal and plastic. My heart sank while my eyes looked to my rearview mirror, and there it was: a larger pickup truck than mine. I had hit it, and I knew I was completely, personally accountable for the accident. There would be no excuse-making because there were none to be made. Yes, we were both backing out, but he was there first, and I had been careless. Insurance rules, regulations, rising rates, and repairs came to my mind, and I thought, *Oh no, what a hassle. I don't need this right now.*

The other driver and I reparked our vehicles and I climbed out. My worries tripled as he extracted himself from his truck. He was in his fifties, with a shaved head, and simply huge. I was certain he had a professional wrestling background. But then he glanced at both trucks and said, "Looks like you took it worse than I did!" I smiled inside, relieved, though still concerned about the conversation to come. I apologized and let him know that I knew the accident was totally "my bad," and waited for his next move. Inspecting the damage to our vehicles more closely, he looked at me, grinned, and said, "Heck, I've hit other people's cars, too. Let's just forget it. No big deal." It was then I realized I had been holding my breath. Exhaling, I reached out, shook his hand (but did not offer my name, lest he change his mind and come find me), and declared, "You're a good man!" As he walked away, though, he looked back and spoke authoritatively: "Now let me back out first!"

Everyone makes mistakes. Even in the best organizations, people sometimes submit the wrong paperwork, add up the numbers incorrectly, ship one customer's product to another, and forget to follow through. That's the reality of life. Yes, it's important that things be done correctly, but it's unrealistic to expect perfection from people. Punishing people, holding grudges, and lashing out in anger when mistakes happen serve no purpose except to poison the work environment for everyone. One fast-growing software firm posted this guiding value on their lobby wall: "We Allow Our People to Make Non-Repetitive Mistakes." The way that reads to me is, "You can make a mistake—*once*. But do it again and you're outta here!"

I know some will argue that we can't just let people run amok, making mistakes anywhere and everywhere, all the time—and they'd be right. Maybe it's best said by Papa John. When chatting with John Schnatter—Papa John himself, founder of Papa John's, the pizza restaurant chain—he shared this: "I've always found that people who struggle are hard on others, but those who do well in life are hard on themselves."

The bottom line is that no one thrives in an organizational culture that is quick to attack people when mistakes are made. An organization like that will never be outstanding. When I backed into my large friend's truck, he essentially said, "There but for the grace of God, go I." Meaning, "It could've been me. We all make mistakes. Let's just let it go." We could all gain from his wisdom. If someone you work with commits an error, forgive, forget, and move on to more important things.

·CHAPTER FOURTEEN·

Compete with Competitors, Not Each Other

The Millers of Colorado have milk and eggs delivered to our door every week. It's a service that was once common across the country and now seems rather quaint, but is a terrific convenience. Every Friday morning, around 4 A.M., a big truck rumbles into our driveway and someone stomps up onto our porch, makes noise grabbing dirty bottles and leaving the new ones, and drives away. We have never met this person, but we did get this note from "Dan the Milk Man" one day:

> Dear Customer: I'm writing to let you know I have been gone from the job for several months. I am devastated over the performance of the driver who took my place. Because of him and some other personnel and

computer changes in the main office which have accounted for many book-keeping errors, over half of my 200 customers have quit us and gone to another dairy. I can't tell you how bad I feel, after delivering for so many years, to see others completely destroy all that I have done.

Some might see Dan's note as a statement of caring, commitment, and customer service—and that may have been his intention—but in reality all it does is blame others. It doesn't say anything about what Dan has done, or plans to do, to make things better. His note represents divisiveness within his organization and shows that he forgot that he and his colleagues are on the same team. Do our paying customers really need to hear and see us fighting—with *each other*?

Now, there can be healthy internal competition, such as when individuals or teams compete to come up with the best solution to a problem or the next great product. But when people inside an organization act, as Dan did, as if colleagues and departments are adversaries, it hurts an organization in every way imaginable. And the sad truth is that it goes on all the time. Groups will refer to other groups within the organization as "they" and "them" or managers will say to their staff, "I know that's what headquarters said to do, but we'll do it our way in the field."

After giving a presentation to one branch of the military, I asked my contact if he felt that another branch—housed at the same facility—might also be interested in the program. With a twinkle in his eye, he said, "Here's the deal, John, people support what they create and attack what they don't." I knew exactly what he meant: "NIH," or "Not Invented Here." People often reject an idea or suggestion just because it originated elsewhere, that is, they didn't "create" it or come up with it themselves. It's a terribly wasteful thing to do, but it's one of the things that happen when we compete internally. As one executive client said, gesturing toward the large window in his corner office, "We work awfully hard every day to remember that the enemy is *out there*." That's the way it should be, because in our complex, competitive, and ever-changing world there is simply no room for competing with one another internally. It's stated in the Bible: "A house divided against itself cannot stand." Nor can it be outstanding.

CHAPTER FIFTEEN

Do What You Promise

Have you ever let someone down? Made a promise and not kept it? I sure have. How easy it is to say, "I'll get that info to you today," and then not follow through. Or promise, "I'll schedule the meeting for Wednesday" and completely forget. Sure, it's human. But one thing we've found inside exceptional organizations is that people do what they say they're going to do. In other words, a promise made is one kept.

When I first got into sales, my new manager, Jim Strutton, surprised me in many ways. One fine thing Jim did was keep his promises, which truly amazed me at the time. You see, where I had worked previously, my boss would say, "We'll get into the conference room and do some training," "I'll be talking to my boss about a raise for you," and, after I announced my resignation, "Let's sit down and talk about why you're leaving. I want to know!"

Not one of those things ever took place.

When Jim became my boss, one of my first assignments was to memorize a key portion of my sales presentation. One Friday, he told me he'd call me the following Tuesday at noon so I could recite that piece to him over the phone. (We couldn't do it face-to-face because his office was a thousand miles away.) Sure enough, at precisely 12 o'clock on the following Tuesday, the phone rang. Picking up, I heard, "John, I'm ready to hear your presentation." I was stunned. I didn't really believe that he'd call, but as I came to learn over the years, when Jim said he'd do something—*anything*—you could trust that he would. And he did.

Most organizations today talk about the importance of teams and teamwork. Ideas such as collaboration and trust-building are taught over and over, and they are critical, for sure. But in so many ways, when we simply support one another by doing what we say we'll do, we've accomplished the same goals.

Whether it's boss to employee, peer to peer, or

corporate to field and vice versa, nobody should ever be surprised when anyone in the organization keeps a promise. Whatever we say that we'll do, we do. When people treat one another like this, outstanding things happen.

CHAPTER SIXTEEN

Hire Character

Rick Beresford has more than thirty years' experience in human resources, training, and talent development—much of it with Wells Fargo. Rick has a special ability to simplify the complicated, and has conveyed many terrific ideas to me. Here's one that you wouldn't think needs to be said: Select the *best* person for the job.

I say—AMEN!—and let's start by hiring character over college degrees.

Ashley is a hardworking twenty-two-year-old college graduate with a bachelor's degree in psychology. She is honest, courteous, respectful, hungry to learn, and *perfect* for the work she wants to do: a Child Life Specialist. As someone who would interact with ill children in a hospital setting, not only does Ashley possess the talent and ability, but kids love her. Ashley to children is like honey to flies, magnets to metal, or a light to a moth.

After volunteering at a hospital for several months, Ashley learned that a position had opened up. Showing initiative, she took her résumé to the Human Resources office by hand (instead of just mailing or emailing it) and left it for the right person. A few days later, she did the right thing: She called to ensure the HR person got it. Then she followed up by phone a week later. Finally, she was informed *by email* that she had not been chosen. When she called to ask for a reason, she was told that the candidate they selected had "more classes and degrees."

They didn't say more experience, nor did they say more skilled. What they said was more classes, degrees—schooling.

The candidate they selected might well be a very fine person and quite capable, too. I don't know him or her, of course. But I know Ashley and can say with confidence the organization made what's become a classic hiring mistake: valuing "book learning" over character.

I shared this philosophy with a client. He thought for a moment and said, "You know, we do hire based on perceived skills, background, and education, but come to think of it, we almost *always* fire on the basis of character, or should I say, the lack of it. We have it backwards."

Character is often described with words such as honesty, courage, integrity. People of character also display, as Ashley did, professionalism, desire, and work ethic. Who wouldn't want people like that on the team? Now, don't get me wrong, if I am going to have brain surgery, I'd prefer the person wielding the scalpel to have a degree. Yet way too often organizations miss out on quality people by applying the wrong criteria.

I've had three mentors in my life: my dad and two gentlemen in the professional world. Neither of the latter two went beyond high school in their formal education, but of one thing I am certain: I would not be what and where I am in life today without the teachings of these men. We are simply off base if we hire and promote based on fancy degrees, school reputations, or how many years someone sat in the classroom. What we should be basing our decisions on—to the extent possible—is what and who the person is deep down.

Outstanding organizations are made up of outstanding individuals, and people of character are, by definition, outstanding individuals. The truth is, the Ashleys of the world are rare. They don't walk through our door every day. So when they do—*hire them!* Find them a position somewhere, somehow, if at all possible. Outstanding organizations don't let good people walk on by or get away. They hire character over credentials.

The best organizations also employ objectivity in the selection process. You'd think that people who make hiring and placement decisions would base them only on what's good for the organization, but sometimes we get so focused on adhering to a policy such as "promoting from within" or diversity—or are swayed by our own personal preferences—that we pass over the best person for the position. Certainly, hiring people is subjective, as we ask, "Will they fit into our culture?" "Can I work with this person every day?" and "Are they really going to be as good as their résumé says they are?"—but way too often we choose people for all the wrong reasons:

They're the owner's brother-in-law.
They attended our college.
My boss likes them.
They already work here and know the culture.

We're in a hurry to fill the job.

They are members of my church or health club.

They're tall. (Don't laugh. It happens.)

This is not to say that the person we do select will fail miserably, just that the opportunity to make the best choice is missed. Outstanding organizations need the best people, not just those who are good enough.

Putting the right person in a position is one of the most powerful things we can do to help our organization be outstanding. Objectively selecting the best person, while choosing character over credentials, is the way to do it.

CHAPTER SEVENTEEN

Believe or Leave

I hopped onto an airport tram early one morn, sat down, flipped open my wireless mini-laptop, and started typing away. I sensed I was being watched, and when I looked up, I saw a middle-aged gent in business attire looking at me intently. I smiled and said, "Good morning." He returned the greeting. I went back to work but could still feel him watching me. Finally, he said, "You must be self-employed." Breaking away from my typo-checking (I do a lot of that), I said, "Yes, I am. But why would you think so?" He responded, "Anyone who works for someone else wouldn't be working so hard."

After we had a chuckle together, I wondered, *Really? Does only an entrepreneurial-type person care, have passion, and love what they do?* I quickly concluded to myself, *Nope. That's one theory I don't buy.*

At a Marriott in Dayton, Ohio, I was escorted to my room by Gerald, the bellman. When we arrived, we entered what I would consider a standard guest room. It appeared clean, bright, and comfortable with all the amenities I need: a bed, a desk, a flat-screen TV, a coffeepot, and plumbing. (When you travel a lot, hotel rooms start to look alike.) Yet all of a sudden, with energy and enthusiasm in his voice, Gerald exclaimed, "Don't you love the new wallpaper—and the drapes, too? Neat, huh? And how about the paint? Real pretty, isn't it? And you'll love our new beds, and the extra outlets for your laptop and cell are a real plus!" Actually, I hadn't noticed any of these things, but I smiled because of something I did notice: Gerald's passion and belief.

People like Gerald have careers, not jobs. They are not *clock* watchers, concerned only with the minutes ticking slowly off the clock each day, but *calendar* watchers, who see the years flying by. Do you know what I mean? If not, just go to any office building on a Monday morning and ride the elevator. You'll hear clock watchers say, "Is it really Monday already?" "Where did the weekend go?" "Boy, is this gonna be a long day!" and "I'll never make it to 'hump day'!" The sad truth is, millions of people hate their

jobs, feel trapped in their careers, or feel underem-
ployed, underutilized, underappreciated, and miser-
able about what they do each day. But then there are
those who look forward to their day, taking great
pleasure and pride in what they do and where they
do it, whether they are doctors, teachers, sanitation
workers—or a hotel bellhop.

In *QBQ!* I say people should "believe or leave,"
and I would love to see an organization use the idea
as a meeting theme. I can just picture a huge "Believe
or Leave!" banner on the wall for all to see as they
come in for their big meeting. This is not about being
judgmental or stifling criticism. The banner wouldn't
say, "Believe or you're a bum!" or "Believe Blindly."
It just means that if you don't believe, it'd be better—
for you and your organization—if you left. Why
would I stay somewhere if I don't believe in the organization and its products, services, values, and mission? If that passion isn't there, I say, *GET OUT NOW!*

A week after I presented at an industrial firm of
one hundred people, I got an email from the owner,
who'd sat in the front row. The "Believe or Leave"
philosophy had been part of my talk, and his note to
me said they'd had four resignations in the days
since my session. *Uh-oh!* I thought, but he went on to

say, "John, this is about the healthiest thing that has happened to us in a long time!" Relieved, I responded with a question: "Would you rather those people had stayed?" To my surprise, he replied, "I wish three of them had, but it's better for people to move on if they don't have passion for this business." Now that's a wise person.

Belief can't be forced on people, either. Doing so only causes problems to be masked, or, worse, leads people into dangerous denial. I remember watching one executive emcee a large meeting at his firm. The company was having severe problems (I knew their struggles because I had already done a team "intervention" or two for the senior group), and this high-energy VP would come up onstage after each speaker finished his or her presentation and bellow into the microphone, "DO YOU BELIEVE?!" The first time, everyone stared. The next time, five people responded. By the fifth "DO YOU BELIEVE?!" there were three hundred people chanting, "YES, WE BELIEVE!" The truth was, they didn't believe—and today the company is no longer in business.

Belief and passion are more than chants or slogans we plaster on the wall. They're what make people excited to get up in the morning and go to work—and no organization can be outstanding without enthusiastic people. Rather than try to manufacture or force belief, we can *build* it daily in ourselves by focusing on the real value we bring to customers and how we make their lives better.

The gentleman on the tram was mistaken. It's not only people who are self-employed who work hard. People everywhere in organizations big and small do so when they believe in what they're doing. I once heard it said that a "zealot" is simply someone who believes in something more than I do. Every organization needs an army of zealots, because it is our passion and belief that propel us forward and help us stand out from the rest. Be a zealot. Life's too short to wait for hump day.

·Chapter Eighteen·

Make No Excuses!

Since 1995, I have written and spoken on a powerful principle: Personal Accountability. And, of course, every single one of the seven Miller children knows that, so sometimes I wonder if they just like to frustrate me.

When Charlene was eleven, she came home from school upset one day, saying that "best friend" Madison had been "bossy, rude, and mean" and had pronounced herself president of the "Cool Crew," a club that Charlene insisted she herself had founded. This is serious stuff in the fifth grade! As I listened to her describe her bad day, she suddenly interrupted herself saying, "And yes, Dad, I know what you're gonna say. I should be more accountable and ask how I can *make Madison be nicer to me*!"

Oh, so close, little one!

Daughter Tara, while a high school senior, came home one weeknight after I'd turned in and typed out a note on my laptop. This is exactly how it looked and read: "Dad, I'm sorry for not calling to let you know I wouldn't be home by ten. I understand things like this can take away the trust you have in me. I won't even make excuses, because I know I need to have PERSONAL ACCOUNTABILITY!"

I remember thinking, *Wow, great note. She really gets it. What a good kid.* Then I saw a P.S. that said: "Of course, there are always reasons if you want to hear them."

Life teaches us all—whether we're a child, a teen, or an adult—that we cannot control what other people say and do, or most events occurring around us. The only thing we really have control over is ourselves. And this is *exactly* why personal accountability is so critical, and why people and organizations who demonstrate accountability stand out.

In truth, there actually *are* reasons things go awry: people make mistakes, the ball gets dropped, stuff happens. Life can be complicated, confusing, and complex. Because of this, any one of us on any given day could go on and on with "reasons." But when we attempt to exonerate ourselves with explanations, all they sound like are excuses—and, of course, that's all they really are. What we need to do, instead, is look to ourselves and ask, "What can I do?" and get to work solving the problem. In other words, practice personal accountability.

Certainly there are situations in life where we pull out the swords of Facts and Logic and wield them mightily in our defense. But when we are tempted to do so in front of anyone we call "customer," we might want to remember the country song that says, "Here's a quarter, call someone who cares." Never forget: The customer does not care to hear our reasons and excuses. Just ask Alan Farnsworth, head of customer service worldwide for Bausch & Lomb. He's been on the receiving end of the better approach and shares it in this story:

> Connecting through the Paris airport, I was on a bus full of travelers heading out for a remote boarding on a distant tarmac. When we reached our plane, we weren't allowed to get out. Instead, an Air France person came onto the bus to let us know the airplane cabin wasn't ready. I wasn't concerned about the

delay since I was not in a hurry, but I could see other passengers getting increasingly annoyed as the minutes passed.

Once we were finally on the plane and settled in, forty minutes behind schedule, the captain came over the speaker. Honestly, I expected the standard, canned, insincere airline spin such as, "Sorry for the delay, but it's due to the late arrival of the incoming aircraft" or some other routine excuse. Instead, here's what the captain said: "I'd like to personally apologize for this delay. It was due to our failure to get the cabin ready on time, and as captain, I am responsible for that. I didn't get the job done. This is inexcusable. Our practices will change to ensure this never happens again, at least not with any team for which I am responsible. This is not typical of Air France, and I hope you won't hold this against us, because we can do better—and you deserve better. Now, please sit back and enjoy the flight. We may be late, but we'll make it as pleasant as possible for you."

I have never heard such honesty like this

in circumstances like these. You should have seen the passengers' response. It was fascinating to observe. Nodding heads, smiles, and faces that clearly said, *OK, that's pretty nice. I feel better now.* People's agitation and irritation seemed to be replaced by acceptance and relaxation. While observing all of this, it occurred to me that candor and accountability like this are exactly how every organization ought to deal with their customers. After experiencing it—after feeling it myself—I know it works!

Question: How complex is it for an airline to get a plane off the ground on time?

Answer: Extremely.

And more often than not, the crew is as frustrated as the passengers. They want to get going, too! But if this Air France pilot had shared "The Five Reasons You Can't Blame Us" with his customers, what would that have accomplished? Nothing positive, that's for sure. So he took the High Road of Personal Accountability and simply said, "No excuses." Outstanding!

Alan's tale is a terrific example of one individual taking responsibility for a problem in a surprising and inspiring way—but that's probably not the whole story. Since individuals often act within the context of their organization and its culture, I can't help but wonder what might have been in the captain's training and the organizational environment that contributed to his behavior.

More important, what can each of us do to engage in the same behavior in our organization?

CHAPTER NINETEEN

Celebrate

What comes to mind when you hear the word *celebration*? Party hats? Fireworks? A parade? How about a five-foot-tall house plant? Remember my manager Jim Strutton, who followed through on his promises? Well, he was also good at celebrating victories, both large and small. I was home alone one day, working in my basement office, when the doorbell rang. By the time I got to the door, the delivery person was gone, but there was an enormous potted plant sitting on my steps. The note attached was from Jim and it was addressed not to me, but to my wife, Karen. Jim's note said how glad he was to have us *both* "on the team," and how proud of me he was for that month's sales performance.

That act of celebration meant a lot to Karen and me. This was my first sales job—I had joined the company just three months earlier—and we were both feeling the pressure of my new position. Jim's gesture spoke volumes about my new boss, his beliefs about recognition and how to treat people. It affirmed for both of us the decision to join this small organization. I could say that Jim's gesture would've been even better had the florist removed the bright red tag that said "Price reduced—50% off." But, hey, it's always good to save a few dollars! The important point is that I knew I was working for a company that valued and celebrated its people.

Now, not all celebration is equal. Many books, training programs, and consultants nowadays talk about having "fun at work," and, sure, it's good to have fun, but work is not really a party, either. It's better to go beyond placing brightly colored "let's remember to have fun" trinkets and stuffed animals on our desks and banners on our walls, and ensure our celebrations are connected to victories.

A celebration is anything that says, *Congratulations! Great job! Yes, we did it!* It could be as simple as a kind word, more formalized like an "employee of the month" award, or as grand as fireworks and a parade. And the victory celebrated could be anything from closing a sale to taking the company public.

Whatever it is, when our celebrations are connected to triumphs, now we're having fun with *purpose*— and the rewards are many. Reveling in the thrill of accomplishment is not only darn exciting, it fills the deep human need for appreciation, belonging, and being part of a team. It also helps people feel they're a part of something larger than themselves, so they're far more likely to be personally invested in their organization and give their all to helping it be outstanding. The opposite of this is what one senior manager whispered to me at a major corporate bank event: "Way too often our people feel like nothing they do is ever quite good enough."

Outstanding organizations celebrate victories. Let's start doing it today.

CHAPTER TWENTY

Be Flexible: Put People Before Policies

Every organization has policies, and most are justified and important. It's also true that a strict, unreasonable adherence to "rules and regs" can sometimes do an organization more harm than good.

I took our ten-year-old malamute husky, Bear, to see our veterinarian, whom we call "Dr. D." He used to be at a different clinic, and we've gone to him for many years, but he's now opened a private practice a mile from our house. It's perfect: pleasant staff, a doc we like and trust, and a handy location.

Before I left the office with Bear, Dr. D. prescribed some pills to control Bear's joint pain. I knew the pills would make her more comfortable, but I was flabbergasted at the price. Once home, I found the exact same item from an online animal pharmacy for 50 percent less! So I called the clinic and reached the gal at the desk whom I had just interacted with in person, and said, "Hi, Amy. I think I'd like to return the tablets I got for Bear. Can I bring them back, please?" Without even asking why, Amy said, "I'm sorry, but we won't take them back." Huh. No questions. No curiosity. No discussion whatsoever. The hair on my neck began to stand up. "How come?" I asked, working to keep a positive tone. "I haven't even opened them, and the seal is unbroken." "Sorry," she retorted, "that's our policy." *Policy?!* In a four-person vet shop that's been open one month and really needs all the customers it can find?

Now, before I go on, this is not a debate over being allowed to return prescription drugs. This is about the cost to any organization that has rigid "That's our policy!" thinking. This almost goes without saying, but the long-term value of the Millers being happy and loyal customers who return again and again while recommending the wonderful Dr. D. to friends and family is worth a whole lot more than the profit margin in that one bottle of pills.

Reverting instantly and robotically to policy causes the customer to feel devalued, dismissed, even distrusted. Was Amy really thinking that I might've tampered with the bottle?! It shuts down conversation and communication. Rather than drawing people toward our organization, it repels them. Furthermore, this blind adherence to policy and all the costs that come with it doesn't happen just with our paying customers.

At nineteen, Casey Mae is a full-time student who played college softball while holding down a part-time job at a coffee shop. One weekend when she was on the other side of the country participating in a softball tournament, she learned they'd be staying an extra day—but she was scheduled to work the next day. Stuck 1,500 miles away, she called her boss to explain her dilemma. Her boss said, "Okay, find your replacement!" Casey Mae did all she could—phoning and texting—to get someone to work her shift. When she couldn't, she promptly informed her manager, who said, "Keep trying." She did, but never found anyone to cover for her, and let her boss know. Though she felt badly about it all, she assumed that was the end of it.

The next time Casey Mae worked, the boss made no mention of the uncovered shift. At the end of the day, her manager approached waving a sheet of paper and said, in a lilting, singsong voice, "Guess what I have for you?" Casey Mae didn't know what it was and her face showed it. "I'm writing you up," her boss continued, "because we were short-staffed last weekend and you didn't get someone to cover your shift." Casey Mae was stunned, not to mention embarrassed and angry. There hadn't been *one* hint that failing to find a sub was anything more than an inconvenience. Now she was being treated as if she'd committed a serious offense. When she asked why, the manager said, "It's policy! If you don't cover your shift, you get written up."

Ironically, this incident actually reveals the *strength* of Casey Mae's character. Organizations search daily for people who demonstrate accountability, work ethic, commitment, and honesty—as she did. Yet because her manager was focused more on the policy than the person, Casey Mae was now on permanent record for "bad behavior," when in reality there had been none. The smarter choice for the manager would've been to *thank* Casey Mae for her efforts, her forthrightness, and her desire to do the right thing. Sadly, that's not the way it was handled, and there are real costs to organizations when they blindly follow rules and regulations. Doing so causes us to forgo those critical opportunities—those precious moments—when we can solve problems, build trusting relationships, and serve people.

I'm not suggesting that Casey Mae's employer should never reprimand people, or that Dr. D. should start taking returns under any circumstances. Yet I do believe reasonableness and old-fashioned common sense are critical to an organization's success and generate far more loyal customers and enthusiastic employees than any policy ever created.

Remember this: Blessed are the flexible, for they keep customers from getting bent out of shape.

Stay flexible.

CHAPTER TWENTY-ONE

Succeed with What You Have

I was walking through the Atlanta airport when I spotted a food kiosk recessed into the wall, offering sandwiches, salads, fruit, desserts, and drinks. I decided to stop and get some lunch, but what really caught my eye was the employee running the operation. She was basically standing out on the concourse with no counter or table to work with, so in order to help a customer she had to engage in an impressive series of maneuvers. As she served the gent ahead of me, I watched while she first hung a plastic "grocery" bag on her left wrist and placed his salad, bottled water, and banana into the bag. Then she turned to the cash register and deftly swiped his credit card, grabbed the receipt, and quickly handed the card and receipt back to the customer—all with her free right hand. Finally, she removed the bag from her wrist and gave the customer his lunch along with a cheery "Thank you very much!" I was impressed with her—and when she spoke, her accent made me wonder where she was from originally.

When it was my turn, I handed her my sandwich, Diet Coke, and carrot cake (not being quite the healthy eater as the guy before me), and the whole routine started again. She put it all in a bag dangling from her arm while swiftly taking my money and processing the transaction.

Seeing how well she managed all this, I offered a friendly observation—maybe I was even teasing her a bit—saying, "Boy, you'd think management could at least give you a small table to put stuff on, eh?!" Without a second's delay, she smiled and said something I don't believe is heard very often: "Oh, that's all right . . . I work with what they give me."

Excuse me? I thought. *Did I hear you right? Did you just say, "I work with what they give me"?* My next thought was, *You really* aren't *from this country, are you?*

Don't get me wrong, the United States is the greatest country in the world to live in. But maybe *because* of our immeasurable, countless, and unending blessings, most of us are so protected from the pain of doing without, that we end up complaining more about what we *don't* have than being thankful for what we *do* have. Here was an employee essentially saying, *I'm glad to be gainfully employed and I will smile at every customer who comes my way because I know they pay the bills. And I won't whine about what I lack!*

No organization is perfect, and few have everything people working there feel they need. Of course, there are times to speak up to express a need for this tool or that resource, and management should do everything it can to provide people with the very best tools available. But as individuals, focusing on what we *don't* have rather than on what we can accomplish with what we *do* have is a waste of time and energy. In the end, outstanding organizations and their people get the job done with the tools and resources they've been given.

CHAPTER TWENTY-TWO

Work!

I asked Molly, our twentysomething daughter, who loves soccer and basketball and has served as captain in both sports, "Molly, in your opinion, what makes an effective team?" I was honestly just curious what she'd say; it wasn't like I was doing serious research for a book or anything! But I loved her answer: "Everyone taking care of their own stuff, Dad. Everybody working hard at doing their job . . ."

That's exactly what happens in outstanding organizations. People do their jobs. They work— diligently. I didn't say they get their life out of balance. I believe in balance and taking breaks and recharging. I didn't say people should shortchange their family in some way. Family is critical. And I didn't say people should become obsessed 24/7 with their jobs, either. But I do say this: In outstanding organizations a solid work ethic is alive and well. People care, contribute, and combine talent and skills with old-fashioned "elbow grease" to get the job done. In lesser organizations, that's not always the case.

There's a phenomenon we all know about called "entitlement thinking." People inflicted with this condition have one mantra—*I deserve!* Outstanding organizations work hard to make hard work a cornerstone of their culture and keep entitlement at bay.

"I deserve!" thinking can look like this:

- A supervisor who felt strongly that the content of a particular book would help each person in his group learn and grow professionally and personally, happily gave one to each of his reports. Everyone was excited! Later, one employee returned to ask, "If I read this book at home on my own time, will I get paid for that hour?"
- An industrial complex was locked down for safety reasons from 10:30 A.M. to 3:30 P.M. There was a deadly threat occurring and management wanted all employees to be secure. People's lives were their first concern. One

week later, an employee submitted a request to be paid for the lunch hour he missed.

- A dozen manufacturing plant supervisors were being trained as facilitators of a training process. They were engaging in a full-day session with no minutes to spare. Lots to do! At 9 A.M., the trainer broke them into three teams of four to do group work in breakout rooms—but nobody went to their breakout room. At 9:05, the trainer located all twelve in the cafeteria eating. When asked what they were doing, one said, "Hey, rules are rules. It was time for our break."

All of these examples speak to the entitlement mentality that chips away at an organization's work ethic. Talking with one client about the dangers of this kind of thinking, she said, "Yeah, whenever someone says to me, 'I've been here three months, when will I get my first raise?' I always respond with, 'Your raise will be effective when *you* are!'" Well, that's one way to handle it.

My daughter Kristin—now a colleague of mine who loves working with audiences, too—and I were speaking in Washington, D.C., a block from the White House. So we did the tourist thing the night before our sessions, and together experienced a moment when someone clearly had the right attitude. I'll let Kristin tell the story:

Getting hungry, we decided to grab some dinner, but most eateries in a nearby food court had already closed. Luckily, we found a Quiznos sandwich shop still open and placed our order a minute or two before the 7:30 closing time with Maria, a woman of about twenty who looked like she'd had a very long day. As we stood back and waited for our sandwiches, a stately, well-dressed, elderly couple approached the counter and started reading the menu. The clock on the wall now read 7:32. The Quiznos employees—including Maria—had started cleaning up for the night. Meanwhile, I felt my own discomfort as the couple stood at the counter, quietly perusing the menu. I so badly wanted to stop them from ordering. "Nooooo! They're closed! See the clock? Let Maria go home! She's tired!" As the time ticked to 7:35, though, the couple stepped forward. Maria happened to turn around right then and noticed them. The couple stood waiting expectantly, and I awaited a confrontation: the inevitable show-down between the employee saying, "Sorry, we're closed" and the customers pleading, "It's only a few minutes past. Can't you make just two more sandwiches?" It never happened. Maria stepped up to the register and even though I saw her peek at the clock, she said, smiling, "Can I help you?" Well, apparently she's no slacker. Some people say the young people of today don't know what it means to work, but I say not true! Maria is evidence of that.

Thankfully, Maria cared enough about her responsibilities and her customers to do the right thing at the right time. Let's each of us do the same. As Molly said, it's about everybody working hard, doing their job. It really does come down to having a good work ethic, and no organization can be outstanding without it.

Let's work!

CHAPTER TWENTY-THREE

Remember, People Want to Win

People do not come to work to fail. They come to be successful. They want to win. When organizations and those who run them forget this, it leads to at least three critical errors.

We try to motivate people.

Motivation exists within people, as does the natural desire to excel. We don't need to artificially infuse motivation into others—nor could we, even if we tried. Many a manager, believing it's their job to motivate others, thinks, *I'm gonna motivate this person till it kills him! I'll* make *him want to succeed!* This is like a parent whose child wants to be a musician, trying instead to make him be a physician. It can't be done, at least not without producing negative consequences in the relationship. Knowing people are created to succeed and the motivation to do so is already in them truly frees managers to work on being the best manager they can be.

Lousy managers, when things are not going well, fall into the trap of blaming people for not caring, not trying, not working hard, and "not being motivated." Instead, they should address not only their own skills, but what surrounds people: the environment. The best managers and organizations focus constantly on the internal climate by providing good tools, training, daily coaching, and the removal of roadblocks that inhibit people from getting the job done. To use a sports term, managers at all levels know it's their job to "run interference," enabling people to succeed every single day because, again, people really do want to.

We build lousy performance management systems.

In some organizations people are not allowed to be outstanding. Valerie, a call-center phone rep for a big box retailer, sat down for her first annual review. In preparation for it, her manager asked her to rate her own performance. This organization uses a five-level rating system with Unsatisfactory at the bottom and Outstanding—yes, *outstanding*—at the top. Reflecting on her performance, Valerie thought, *Well, I've worked hard, learned the company's processes, devel-*

oped the skills needed, not had one single "needs improve-ment" pointed out to me, and have been praised by my boss for a year! So she rated herself Outstanding. During the review, though, her manager said, "I'm sorry, nobody can achieve an 'Outstanding' rating." *What?* No one is *ever* rated "Outstanding"? If people aren't allowed to achieve it, why have it as part of the ratings system at all? The message sent is: *No matter how well you perform, in our eyes, you're merely adequate.* There might be compensation and human resources explanations for this that I am not aware of, but to look at an achiever and basically say, "You can't win here" is a really poor way of rewarding people for great work. In fact, it's no reward at all.

When I shared Valerie's story with a client who is an HR director, he said, "We finally did away with the annual performance appraisal process. Direct reports now have at least quarterly meetings with their managers to review performance and development progress." Very smart. They recognize that people can't get the feedback required to improve if they are only given it once a year. That'd be like a parent informing their child one time every 365 days how he or she is turning out—and every parent knows how ridiculous that would be. Outstanding organizations build performance management systems that make sense—and help people succeed.

We lose our top performers.

Deanna, a human resources director with a pharmaceutical firm, confided to me, "John, we've built a culture here where average-performing employees feel safe, comfortable, and stay forever, but the best ones get out." Her organization is not alone. Top performers like to win—and love the perks that come with winning, such as recognition from management, status within their group, higher income, and deep feelings of accomplishment. If organizations don't allow top performers to be top performers, and reward them accordingly, they'll walk right out the door—yes, they will fire their employer—and go somewhere else.

On my way to a meeting, I was lost. I dialed the company and I'll never forget the woman who answered. Her name was Stephanie. With both joy and warmth in her voice (on a Monday morning, no less), Stephanie asked if I would hold. "No problem," I said. After a couple minutes, I was just about to hang up when she came back on and said, "Mr. Miller, are you still there?" "Yes I am," I said, and then came the words I've never forgotten:

"I'm so thankful you held for me!"

Wow, I thought, *those are some powerful words.*

"That's fine," I said. While she gave me directions, I was thinking about her choice of words. *Thankful?* She said she was thankful I had held for her, and I could tell she was. And by acknowledging my patience and thanking me as she did, she made me feel pretty special. When I arrived, I couldn't wait to meet her—and I wasn't disappointed. Not only did she offer me a gracious welcome, but she was also friendly, upbeat, and energetic.

After getting settled in the lobby, I walked over to the reception counter, leaned across, and spoke quietly. "Stephanie, if this organization is not careful, somebody is going to steal you away." She smiled, lowered her voice, and said, "Someone already did. Today's my last day!"

No surprise there. Someone spotted her talent and lured her away. When I met with her CEO minutes later, he asked rhetorically, "Why can't we get good people?" *Hmm,* I thought, *there's one walking out your door today.*

But it isn't only about the best people leaving. It's also about who stays behind. People live up to our expectations of them. When our culture is based on the view that people don't want to win, we get more people who don't want to win. Mediocrity sets in and becomes the standard. But when we view every person as one who wants to be their best, not only do we keep our stars, more people rise to their potential.

In your organization, look hard at how people are being managed, at the environment and the existing performance management systems, as well as how top people thrive—or don't. Study it all, and make the changes needed to ensure that the organizational culture embraces the truth that people don't come to work to fail. Let them win—because they really do have the motivation to do so!

CHAPTER TWENTY-FOUR

Never Forget Who Pays the Bills

Do you ever imagine how things could be? I do, though not so much about changing the world or what it'll be like when I reach some big goal. My dreaming is often about . . . well, how things ought to be.

First, the reality part of the story: It was 8:57 on a Saturday morning. I was standing in front of what the Miller kids call a "haircut store." I needed a trim, but waiting forty-five minutes in a busy hair salon on a weekend to get one is not one of my life goals. So, as I always do, I arrived just before they opened at 9 A.M. And then, surveying the parking lot and seeing how many other people had a similar idea, I slipped out of my truck and went to lean on a pillar in the store's entryway, trying to look casual and not too obsessed with being first in line.

At 8:58, I noticed a woman hurrying along the sidewalk toward me with key in hand. She came right up to where I was, did not acknowledge me, put her key in the salon door, unlocked and opened it just a bit, and then quickly squeezed through the newly created opening. When I moved to follow her, she turned and curtly said, "We're not open yet," and proceeded to shut and relock the door from the inside—right in my face.

That's when I began to dream.

"Good morning, sir! Wow, so, *so* good to see you! Isn't it just a fine Colorado day? And it's not just about the weather—it's about *you*, because *I* know why you're here. You've come to fork over some hard-earned cash so that my colleagues and I can pay our bills, put food on our tables, and send our children to college. *You*, sir, at this moment, are *the most important person in my world!* We open in a few minutes. Would you like to come in and have a seat while you wait? Do you like coffee, sir? Great, I'll get a pot brewing right away. Welcome!"

Wouldn't that have been terrific? That's the sort of thing I dream about: organizations treating their customers like they're the most important people in the world. Unfortunately, for too many organizations—like my haircut store—it's only a dream. And the woman who shut and locked the door on my nose? She was *the manager*!

In *Flipping the Switch*, I suggest that service—*real service*—is simply doing for others that which we don't *have* to do. And it's true: Whenever a customer is absolutely delighted, it's because someone did something for them that they didn't have to. Organizations have spent untold dollars, time, and energy on customer service training, and yet all we really need to do is follow this simple—and profound—idea. Keeping it in mind will help each of us remember to go above and beyond for the people who pay our bills.

The salon manager didn't *have* to let me in, and, of course, she didn't. But think of the impression it would have made on me if she had.

Whether it's a nonprofit working with donors, a church and its parishioners, a government entity serving citizens, or a corporation moving products around the world, we all have customers and without them, no organization would exist. I know that may seem like an obvious thing to say, but it's easy to forget sometimes, especially for those individuals who are higher up or deeper inside the organization and don't deal directly with customers each day. But here's the deal: Outstanding organizations never forget *who pays the bills.*

Who pays *your* bills? Whoever it is, visualize them as wearing a flashing neon sign around their neck with twelve-inch-high letters that read MAKE ME FEEL IMPORTANT!—and then do something for them you don't have to do.

CHAPTER TWENTY-FIVE

Manage!

Question: How many books have been written on leadership?

Answer: Too many.

So often in training classes, boardroom gatherings, three-day seminars, and "lunch and learns," someone brings up a question for discussion, and it's this: What is more important to our organizational success, management or leadership? I bet you can guess which one people tend to choose. Right, *Leadership*. "I want to be a leader!" people exclaim. Programs are titled "Moving from Manager to Leader," as if being a manager means you're not quite there. We are simply obsessed with the idea of leadership. Not that there's anything wrong with leadership, of course. Good leadership is certainly important to an outstanding organization, and for some it speaks of innovation, big-picture thinking, and defining the course to be taken. The problem is, we are always lifting up leadership at the expense of management. People say, "Managers manage tasks, but leaders lead people," and "Management is doing things right, but leadership is doing the right things."

But what those aspiring leaders don't know is that when people describe their boss as a good leader and then are asked to articulate specifically what that person *does* to lead, this is what we hear:

> My boss communicated what I should do.
> He talked to me—and listened.
> When I got it right, she praised me.
> He told me when I was off track.
> I was trained and coached.
> She spent time with me.
> He showed me respect.

Guess what? Every item listed above is a *people management* skill. These are the things effective managers do, day in and day out, with and for their people. It's time to stop glorifying leadership over management. I have yet to find a boss anywhere who was described as a "great leader" who wasn't first a terrific manager of his or her staff.

If you've been awarded a supervisory position of any kind, congratulations! You're in a perfect position to help your organization be outstanding. Now, get rid of all the *I'm a Leader Because I Climbed a Mountain* books and learn to be the very best manager possible. Then, when your team praises you for your amazing leadership, you'll know it's really just about managing people—and managing them well.

CHAPTER TWENTY-SIX

Stand Behind Your Stuff

My wife, Karen, and I went out on a Saturday morning and bought a piece of furniture called a sofa table. Not fancy, but a nice, handsome oak piece. Naturally, it didn't come assembled and ready to go, but in a box, tied with straps, and wrapped with protective material. Well, I hate having an undone project before me, so after we lugged the heavy thing from the back of my truck through the garage into the entry hallway, up twelve steps and onto the living room floor, I went to work. I removed the wooden pieces and metal hardware, grabbed some tools, and began ignoring the instructions—my usual approach. I was doing just fine, for a while. The piece had eight legs, each labeled with a color-coded sticker. Some legs went on this way, others went on that way. Feeling confident (I can color-coordinate with the best of them), I was cruising! Until one leg didn't fit. It looked the same as the others but the screw holes were in the wrong place. It seemed I had an extra blue-labeled leg, not the red one I needed. It'd been mislabeled and was not going to fit. So after spending a few minutes in disbelief and denial, contemplating the question, "Should I grab my drill and make new holes?"—foolish, but still an option I considered—I called the furniture store. Located fifteen miles from our home, I looked forward to hearing, "Not a problem, sir. So sorry to inconvenience you. Since we know how valuable your time is, we'll have someone get the correct leg right out to you. Would noon work, sir?"

Unfortunately, that's not exactly how it went. I got the floor salesperson who'd sold us the table on the phone, and he robotically spoke these words: "Pack it up and bring it back." *Um, excuse me? Undo all that I have done, bind it up, get it back in the box, load my truck, and drive thirty miles round-trip—all for one missing leg?!* That's what I was thinking, but I only said, "Can't someone deliver the leg to me, please?" Well, that request didn't go far, so I asked for a supervisor, and he said "No" even more firmly. So, out of options, I went to work—taking it all back!

When I got home later, walking through my garage, I noticed a piece of paper on the floor. Picking it up, I saw it had fallen from the sofa table carton earlier and was titled, "FURNITURE PICK-UP INFORMATION." Skimming it, my eyes landed on point #3, which read: "While it happens infrequently, an incorrect or damaged item could be shipped to us by our vendor. It is your responsibility to return any imperfect or incorrect product for exchange." So, not only do they not stand behind their products, and blame their suppliers, and shift all accountability to the *customer* for solving problems—THEY PUT IT IN WRITING!!!

I think organizations can do better, and I don't think I am alone.

Jason Ragan, a *Flipping the Switch* reader, found an organization that does do better, and he just couldn't wait to email us about it:

I bought a used Timex watch from an online reseller that included GPS. It was practically new and worked like one right out of the box. But a couple of months later the button used to pick up the GPS signal stopped functioning. I have to admit that I had dropped it and the plastic casing cracked. So I decided to send the watch to Timex to fix it. I saw on their website they promised to repair and return it within 14 days. One problem: I had no proof of purchase since I had bought it used and it was out of warranty. I sent it anyway. Three weeks later I still did not have it back, so I called Timex. The phone rep told me they had mailed it to my P.O. box, but it had been returned to them. So I provided my street address and they promised to ship it out again. I had it within days, but . . . it wasn't my watch. They'd sent me a brand-new one! I couldn't believe it. However, as I was digging around in the box looking for the paperwork, I started feeling a little bummed, thinking, *I don't want to pay for a new watch.* Then I found a note that said Timex apologized for not being able to fix my watch and for failing to get it back to me in a timely fashion. It said this new one was mine to keep—for free! I was only billed for the shipping. How awesome is that? A $300 watch at no charge! And an apology, which truly wasn't needed. They now have a customer for life—and a very vocal advocate for their products—all because of their fine service. Simply put, they went way beyond my expectations.

Two organizations. Two responses to a customer with a problem. Two very different outcomes. Certainly, every organization must decide for themselves how far to go to stand behind their products and services, but here's the key point: The next time Jason needs a watch, the odds are high he'll go straight back to Timex, and the next time the Millers need furniture, the chances are we'll shop around. So, which organization deserves the moniker "outstanding"? I think we all know.

CHAPTER TWENTY-SEVEN

Develop Managers

My dad, "Coach Jimmy," discovered that his best wrestlers did not always make the best coaches. Generally, the better coaches had been mediocre grapplers. When champions became "Coach" they struggled *to* coach for several reasons: Their egos drove them to want to still be the star; they couldn't teach to others what they had done so naturally; they had an extreme lack of patience; and, of course, they had no specific training for this new role. One day an individual team member, the next day in charge of other wrestlers. Overnight they'd become *The Boss*.

Organizations do the same thing all the time—promoting top-performing individual contributors to "manager"—and it often goes badly, mostly because of no management training. Truly, managing others is a whole different skill set from developing software or paying invoices or answering questions on an employee hotline or keeping systems running or selling products and services. When managers aren't trained, and thus don't understand the management job, there are many consequences—one being that good people go right out the door.

Additionally, organizations make the mistake of promoting people to manager simply because they're available. In the words of one client, "If you've been around long enough and are able to fog up a mirror stuck under your nose, you get to be the manager!" The problem is, maybe the person promoted can *never* be an effective manager due to a total lack of potential, no matter how much training they're given. Promoting people beyond their capability has a negative impact on a couple of levels: The move hurts the people now being managed, *and* the organization has lost a solid individual contributor. It'd be better to leave some people right where they are.

Outstanding organizations don't make errors like these; they move the right people up and then train them to do their new and critical job well. They help people transition from player to coach. They recognize that not training managers is a cost that won't show up as a line item on any balance sheet—nowhere will it say "Cost of Not Training Managers"—but that cost is there nonetheless, and it is significant.

CHAPTER TWENTY-EIGHT

Let Every Player Count

After I was done speaking to the U.S. Army in Columbia, South Carolina, Major Jamie Fidler was kind enough to give me a ride to the airport. Along the way, I learned that he loves coaching youth football. Well, he loves the sport and the kids—the parents can be a hassle. Every parent thinks their youngster is the best and the most talented, of course, and they should have a glamour job like quarterback or wide receiver so they can be making the big plays. But when Junior gets assigned a less glamorous position, mom, dad and even grandparents whine and complain, saying things like, "What!? He's *only* a guard on the offensive line!?"

Whenever Jamie gets this sort of grief from the adults he always tells them the same thing: "Your son has a cornerstone job on this team and is critical to our success. You may not be telling him this, but I am going to let him know every single day that we cannot win unless he does his all-important job well."

When I complimented him on his excellent coaching philosophy, he said, "Thanks, but it's pretty simple: Every player counts."

Do you remember in your middle and high school years how there were cool kids—and then everyone else? And the cool kids seemed pretty self-important, while everyone else felt left out, or that they didn't matter much? Organizations shouldn't have "cool kids." We can't afford to have any of our people feel that they don't count.

The fact is, every person in an organization plays an essential role in that organization's success, even though some have more responsibilities, grander titles, and bigger offices than others. Picture high-level executives with broad and far-reaching positions trying to do their jobs without everyone else doing theirs. Whether it is the receptionist managing phone calls, the IT person keeping the systems running, or the maintenance crew maintaining the building's air conditioning and heating, that exec fails without these people doing their cornerstone jobs.

In outstanding organizations people feel personally invested. Jamie tells his players, "We cannot win unless you do your job well." We need to send the same message to all of our people and treat them like the essential players that they are.

No cool kids. Every player counts.

CHAPTER TWENTY-NINE

Speak Well: Make the Right Impression

People have perceptions of organizations. Where do those impressions come from? Almost entirely from how they are spoken to by people representing the organization. And as far as customers are concerned, the people with whom they interact *are* the organization. Have you experienced any perception-shaping moments like these?

- Suffering from severe headache pain, the HMO member calls the emergency line and leaves a message. Two hours later he hears this from the nurse who returns his call: "Sir, we have up to four hours to get back to you."
- At a noisy fast-food place, the customer seeks to clarify the price by repeating the amount

back to the counter person, who snaps, "That's what I said!"

- After waiting an hour in line at a government office, the citizen hands the paperwork to the clerk, who, after a quick glance, says loudly enough for all to hear: "You did this completely wrong. Go back and do it over."
- The church usher spots a couple—who just happen to be first-time visitors—opening a side door to enter the sanctuary, and declares, "Wrong door!" while sternly directing them to doors in the lobby.
- When asked by the restaurant patron who's waited forty-five minutes to be seated, "Do you know when our table will be ready?" the hostess responds, "We did give you a pager, didn't we?!"
- The hotel manager, interacting with a guest who's frustrated about charges on her bill for services she never requested, asserts, "We don't make mistakes like that here."
- A school janitor sees parents entering the building on a rainy, muddy day and barks, "Hey, I just mopped that area!"

- A donor of clothes and toys for the needy backs her minivan up to the nonprofit's door to unload and a staffer yells, "Hey, lady, you can't park there!"
- After enduring thirty-three minutes on hold, the airline customer vents to the phone agent about the wait and is curtly informed, "We're busy."

It just baffles me that it seems to be so difficult for some people to speak kindly, respectfully, and helpfully. What can possibly explain people treating people in such negative ways? Why would anyone risk making a bad impression for their organization by choosing the wrong words and/or employing the wrong tone? At best, the impression created is one of indifference. At worst, we drive people away.

Certainly, individuals are personally accountable for their actions, but the organization plays a role in all this, too—and ignoring that role is a mistake. There are three areas that outstanding organizations constantly address so they can continue to enhance the market's view of them.

SETTING THE STANDARD

Outstanding organizations have standards for how people interact with *all* customers, inside and outside their walls—and they really understand it all starts internally. When managers speak to their staff with words and tone that show respect and kindness— and colleagues do the same with colleagues—then the bar has been set. When discourteous, demeaning, and dismissive behavior is not tolerated internally, people are far more apt to extend this high standard of how to treat people to those on the outside.

HIRING THE RIGHT PEOPLE

Idea: Let's stop putting people with poor relationship skills, no manners, and a total lack of empathy in service positions. Yes, this seems self-evident but this mistake is made all the time. Organizations need employees who radiate empathy, courtesy, and joy. We need people who have the ability to blend helpfulness and humility, while wrapping it all in an attitude of "I'm so glad you're here!" This may be easier said than done, but the best organizations find a way to recruit and hire people like this—and every person who comes in contact with them feels the difference.

TRAINING AND COACHING PROPERLY

Speaking to people in the right way is a skill that can be learned. Each of the aforementioned perception-creating examples could easily be rephrased with new words and retooled for better tone through training and moment-to-moment coaching. The boss's all-important job is to be present to guide people so they learn to say and do the right things in the right way. The goal is for *all* "insiders" to treat all "outsiders" well. A customer should never have to ask for the manager in order to win respect. It should start with the very first person with whom they interact. As Rod Blunck, an executive in public education, says, "Courtesy is free; extending a pleas-ant word costs us nothing. So why not freely give it away?"

I bet if I asked you which organizations you think are outstanding, you'd identify those that spoke well to you. Even if the reason you're talking to them is that they made a mistake of some sort, the fact that they treated you respectfully ended up making a bigger impression—and now you think of them as outstanding. On the other hand, what are the chances you'd mention one of the organizations from our list above? Right, I thought so. In fact, if you were on the receiving end of one of those negative interactions, you might just fire them!

No matter how we see ourselves, it's what our *customers* think that's important. And how we speak to them is what tells them whether we are outstanding—or not. Let's make sure we speak well and make the right impression.

CHAPTER THIRTY

Choose to Change

As the newly appointed superintendent of a large school district in Thornton, Colorado, and a recent arrival from Michigan, Mike Paskewicz was speaking to his principals and deans on his first day on the job: "I won't waste your time telling you what we always did in Detroit," he said, "if you won't keep telling me, 'This is how we've always done it in Denver.'" Mike gets it. He knows that organizations need to move forward rather than looking back—in other words, to change—and that the key to that is in changing the way we think.

Rather than being held back by rigid thinking and resistance to change, outstanding organizations recognize that change is going to happen anyway, whether people like it or not. Products and services move from being newcomers to established brands.

Departments that started with a few people grow into full divisions. Companies go from startup to going public to earning their place in the Fortune 500. Conversely, established brands lose their luster and fade away, divisions and subsidiaries get sold off, and "successful" companies disappear. Economies go up and down. Competitors come and go—and come again. Outside the business world, churches that start in living rooms grow to "mega" status, while school districts that are flat in student population for years experience growth that nobody predicted. Nonprofits founded by someone in their garage with a personal passion suddenly have large staffs that need to be managed, requiring systems that need to be built.

Given the organic, constant, and inevitable nature of change, how could we ever think that what works today will work tomorrow? The reality is, if a strategy or tactic is working now, the odds are high that it *won't* work in the future. There is just too much change taking place in our world for it to be any other way.

Many organizations talk about "best practices" when what should be talked about is "best thinking," because it's our *thinking* that drives our actions, which over time become our practices. Rather than fearing change, outstanding organizations come to see change as a good thing—as necessary and even exciting. They understand that even though there is often pain involved in change, it's far less than the pain that comes from never changing at all. So, not only do they accept and adapt to change, but they also go the extra critical step of *accelerating* change. Simply put, outstanding organizations take charge of change by changing themselves first. For they know that, otherwise, change will happen *to* them—and if that happens, it might just be too late.

·Chapter Thirty-one·

Have the Right People
Make the Right Decisions

As I was driving along a Colorado highway, my cell rang. Clicking on my hands-free unit, I said, "Good morning. This is John Miller!" and almost before I could finish my greeting, I heard a high-energy female voice say, "Hi. I need to train our managers and would like to buy your program." Certainly, to every person who has ever sold anything anywhere, those are words that ring beautifully. So I said, "That's terrific!" and began asking questions, the first being, "What's your name and who are you with?" She said, "Gayle Perryman. I'm with Head Start." (I knew right away that Head Start is a government group that supports low-income families). We began to explore her group's needs, along with timing for implementation, logistics, and The Big Question: investment. I gave her a quote, which she said fit into their budget (more music to a salesperson's ears). I then realized I hadn't asked a key question. "I'm sorry, Gayle," I said, "I forgot to ask what your position with Head Start is."

"Oh," she replied, "I am the director for our county."

I instantly thought, *Wow, and you called* personally *to secure this training for your team? I am impressed!* You see, calling on organizations now for decades, I have been amazed, frustrated, and sometimes disappointed over who gets put into a buying position. There are some things a receptionist should be able to purchase and some things only an executive should buy. Quite honestly, a senior vice president should probably not be ordering copier paper, pens, and coffee for the lobby. Not because it is beneath them, but because their time should be invested in bigger, broader decisions. Conversely, an executive assistant—even though we all know they rule the world—shouldn't be tasked with investigating a possible purchase that will have an impact on the entire organization's culture, like training and development.

The only product and service I have ever sold is learning—training programs, speaking events, public seminars, consulting, and books—so this is the only area I can speak to. But I can tell you, I've had more people than I can count without the authority—or the expertise—sent to contact me to explore what we offer. I've even had twenty-two-year-old summer interns call or email. They're good people, I'm sure, but the *wrong* people to be put into this position. When this happens, it stresses out both them and the supplier, and generally distorts the information that the "real buyer" needs to receive and understand.

Certainly, a sales vice president would not purchase a piece of manufacturing equipment, just as a plant manager would not choose an incentive program for field sales reps. Taking this idea a step further, the plant manager would not buy a machine for the assembly line without involving the people on the plant floor who will be using it. The people who get actively involved in buying decisions should have the appropriate knowledge, experience, and authority.

In my sales career, I have presented to lots of "buying committees" consisting of six or eight or ten or more people. Before I would tell them what I was offering, I learned that if I asked each person, "What is your purpose today in this meeting?" some would rightly say, "To decide on this training option." Others would look at me like I had just landed from another planet, answering, "Um, I don't know. I was just told to be here." This costs an organization in two ways: short-term, having people in meetings who don't need to be there is a waste of time and money; long-term, it results in slower and poorer decisions.

Gayle at Head Start understands exactly what I am saying. When I expressed surprise and pleasure over her calling that day, she said, "Why wouldn't *I* be the one to call you?" In other words, she knew that when acquiring something that can and will influence an entire organization, this is not the time to abdicate her responsibility by handing the decision-making off to someone else.

Let's make sure the right people are making the right decisions.

CHAPTER THIRTY-TWO

Elevate the Conversation

In organizations, people need to *talk* to one another. Sounds obvious, I know, but sometimes there are groups, teams, or departments that just do not communicate with one another very well—even when they're in the same room! And even in our high-tech world of virtual meetings, webcasts, and online chats, getting people together still brings tremendous value. Being face-to-face is a fundamental human need that isn't going away just because we've come up with time- and money-saving meeting options. The desire to know our teammates better, to understand their views, and to be connected to them is a powerful one, and it's still best done in person. And since there is less face time available than ever before—at least in most organizations—it's even *more* imperative that the time invested in a gathering be both productive and constructive.

When I first started working with teams, I remember how odd it seemed that people didn't speak up or communicated in "code," failing to address real problems. Over time, I began to see that there are four levels of conversation or communication among teams and work groups. "Team talk," if you will, ranged from nonexistent to truly healthy, valuable, and meaningful. I call these levels the "4 D's" and here they are:

DENIAL

To call this lowest level "conversation" is really a misrepresentation because there is no talking or communication going on at all. Colleagues, teams, and organizations that are in *Denial* simply see no problems. And since they believe that all is well, there's nothing really substantial to talk about. The truth is, there are always problems, always ways to improve. If people aren't talking about them it's either because they aren't speaking up, complacency has set in, or everyone is speaking in so much code, the problems are being masked. Whatever the cause, *Denial* is not a good place to be. We could almost call this level of noncommunication "Dysfunction Junction," and teams who live there don't get much done.

DEBATE

The next level up is *Debate,* and it is an improvement over *Denial,* but not by much. The good news with this level is that problems are now being recognized, and people accept that they should be searching for solutions. The bad news is, the objective of any debate is to win. When the goal of a conversation is to defeat the other person, it's not going to be a very healthy talk. Some people are so competitive they want to "win" even if it hurts the group. The truth is that we should never make the individual more important than the organization, and when people debate possible solutions to problems with the only objective being to take home the Talking Trophy, everyone loses.

Inherent in any debate is the concept that one

person must be right while another is wrong—and right way/wrong way thinking stifles the problem-solving process. With lots of issues there are many shades of gray. Seeing problems only in black and white keeps us from getting to the root of the problem and, more important, from coming up with an effective solution. And only when we find solutions do we all win.

DISCUSSION

This next level of conversation is where we begin to get somewhere. With *Discussion*, problems have not only been acknowledged and brought into the light, but people are also more willing to set aside personal agendas and their need to be right in order to solve the problem. Willfulness, defensiveness, and competition recede, while interaction moves toward collaboration.

The word "collaborate" literally means working (*labor*) together (*co*). So at this level, the conversation is less about people, personalities, and personal goals, and more about solving problems—as a team. Sounds better, doesn't it? *Discussion* is a pretty good place to be, but it's still not as good as our fourth and highest level. . . .

DIALOGUE

In *Dialogue*, the conversation goes beyond simply talking about problems and how to fix them to working together in an honoring and respectful way. People are listening to one another—and hearing and understanding. There is a kindred spirit that says, *We're all in this together. What can be done to solve this problem?* In *Dialogue*, people want to find the solution—and they don't care who or where it comes from.

At this level, even people's body language is different. There are no defensive postures, such as crossed arms, fidgeting, scowls, or rolling eyes. Colleagues are facing one another, leaning forward, nodding their heads, making good eye contact, physically demonstrating a desire to understand, to grasp what the other person is saying. There's a palpable openness in the room, even laughter. *Dialogue*, more than any of the other D's, is a fun place to be. For most people, it is gratifying to understand, to be understood, to create, and to build—and to solve the darned problem!

Now, in reflecting on the 4 D's, the goal for any team is to be in *Dialogue* as often as possible. How do we get there? Take some time, sit down with your team, and explore each level. Use their responses as a measure. Honestly rate your group against the four D's. At what level do your conversations typically occur? What's preventing the team from moving higher? What can each person do to help elevate the conversations? And lastly, when we reach the fourth D—*Dialogue*—what will be the benefits to us all?

CHAPTER THIRTY-THREE

Fire Customers! (If Necessary)

Standards exist in all organizations for service, quality, safety, dress, performance, and more. I suggest there should also be a standard for how people are allowed to be treated—*by the paying customer.* I said in the introduction to this book that people fire companies. Well, outstanding organizations are willing to fire customers, too. Yes, sometimes *customers* need to be fired.

The world's largest coffee beverage chain had one such customer. This gentleman would visit various stores and ask for a "Venti Americano," which has four shots of espresso and water. But then he would ask for the water to be replaced with soy milk. Well, any barista worth her salt knows that this is technically no longer an Americano but a latte, and the second it becomes a latte, the required number of espresso shots drops from four to two. So, what he was *really* asking for was a "Venti quad soy latte," which is more expensive than a standard latte, which is more expensive than the Americano he wanted to pay for in the first place. Clear as mud? Bottom line, he was trying to cheat the system and get the soy milk and extra two shots of espresso for free.

Along with his attempts to get something for nothing, he was also abusive to the staff. Belligerently, he would make a scene, arguing with the baristas in a rude and disrespectful manner. Since this was happening at several stores, the district manager caught wind of it. Soon after, she sent an email to all stores with a description of the customer and instructions that he was no longer welcome and not to be served anymore.

She fired the customer, and I say, Bravo! Not only is it the right thing to do—abusive behavior should not be tolerated under any circumstances—but her action speaks volumes about the organization's culture. It sends terrific messages to the people, such as we care about you, you're important, and we will stand up for you.

The truth is, in spite of the platitudes we've heard to the contrary, the customer is *not* always right.

Sometimes they are rude, selfish, mean, and their behaviors devalue an organization's staff. Yes, every organization needs to mind its bottom line and define
this important boundary for itself, but standing up
for our people in the face of mistreatment by customers makes our staff feel truly valued. It means a
lot to people to belong to an entity that has standards
like that.

CHAPTER THIRTY-FOUR

Train

Since 1986, the field of training and development has been my profession and passion. I am convinced that outstanding organizations help their people grow through formalized training processes—while others do not. Organizations that don't train find many excuses not to institute training. The big one, of course, is tied to money, as in the following email that I received from a midlevel manager at a large food manufacturer:

> Our corporate office started a program to collect money-saving ideas from employees, so I submitted a recommendation online that we should do more training to make people more efficient and effective at their jobs. I also said that we shouldn't be cutting training budgets

but rather expanding them. Lamentably, I received the following response:

Your "Great Idea" submission will not be implemented due to the following reason: Cost analysis has shown that the idea proposed would have Insufficient Return on Investment.

Thank you for your valuable contribution, and please continue to send us your great ideas!

Your "Great Ideas" Committee

Unfortunately, training is all too frequently viewed as a discretionary expenditure. Training dollars usually are the last budgeted and the first cut. It can be an incredible uphill climb to get some executives to make the investment without "proof that it will work." This type of thinking stems from organizations buying into what I call *The Big Lie*, which is this: The return on dollars invested in training can be precisely measured. This untruth then becomes *The Grand Excuse* for not investing in training at all.

Honestly, there is no way to predict what a seminar, national sales meeting, or team intervention will bring in additional revenue, productivity, or profit—and anyone who claims they can with their surveys, statistical models, and pie charts is blowing smoke. But that doesn't mean training isn't a good investment. Training goes to the very heart of what makes an organization outstanding. It creates team members who are sharp, able, and ready to solve problems, while building trust, loyalty, and confidence—not to mention competence. It equips people with the skills and knowledge they need to succeed, while providing organizations the competitive edge required to thrive in any market environment. Good training does all this and more—but it still can't be measured, at least not in the way we measure other investments.

Why do some organizations seek out training in the first place? Well, it is not because someone woke up one day and decided their per employee work output was down "X%" or sales were off even more. In truth, organizations that seek training have observed how people behaved and, based on the anecdotal evidence they gathered, concluded that training was needed. The driving "metric" in their decision is not a financial or productivity statistic—it is their "gut." So if gut feelings and anecdotal evidence are sufficient to *identify* the problem, then they're also appropriate measures for the solution. The effectiveness of training is gauged by changes in the behavior and actions of the employees, and this is evidence we can readily spot with our eyes and ears. When we can see the change in people that the training was designed to achieve, then we are seeing positive results.

Also, look at what the "professionals" do: Doctors, nurses, pilots, engineers, accountants, among others, require continuous training and education—and not because of a forecasted quantifiable financial return. Learning is necessary to stay current, confident, and competent in a continually changing world. Outstanding organizations consider everyone from salespeople to middle managers to team leaders to executives as professionals, and so they train them. In the end, the organization that views their people as professionals and trains them accordingly has the more professional people.

Here is a lesson the marketplace has taught me: Organizations that don't train because an "ROI" cannot be forecasted don't really believe in training. One cannot say, "I believe in training people!" and in the same breath ask, "What will our money earn?" Investing in training and development is a decision made on a core belief in training; it is not a decision made on numbers.

Truly, we must train people to be outstanding. That does not mean, however, that we should just do *any* training—and we certainly shouldn't implement poor training. In defense of the executives who are reluctant to fund training, they've seen a lot of lousy programs because there's a ton of junk on the training market. However, training that pays off *can* be acquired—or developed—if we know what to look for. A training process that works meets seven key criteria. Using the acrostic PROCESS, these seven characteristics are:

> **P**ractical Content: Excellent content is practical content—and content is only practical when it helps people know *what* to do (Concepts and Principles), *how* to do it (Techniques and Methods), and *why* they should do it that way (Purposes and Reasons). When participants get involved in great material, they'll give the training experience the best compliment possible: "Thanks! It was practical!"— which means they can use it, that it will elicit

action *and* behavioral change. That, of course, is precisely the purpose of training in the first place.

In 1990, Craig Palmer attended a management training project that I facilitated. Two decades later, during one of our periodic phone chats, I asked, "Hey, Craig, remember the material we went through in that session years ago . . . ?" and before I could finish, he responded, "Remember? I still use it every day!" This is not a haughty boast by a man who now at sixty years young is a vice president of sales for a medical device firm. Nor is it overwrought pride on my part for the program. It simply shows the long-term impact and value of well-designed, commonsense content.

Repetition: The motor of learning is repetition. If there is no way to repeat the training, then most likely it will fail. One exposure isn't enough. People need repetition in order to successfully navigate the four stages of learning.

When first exposed to a new idea, we become *aware* of it; we now know it exists. Then, as we try it, we feel *awkward*—and this is where most people quit trying. Gradually, though, if we keep applying the idea, we attain a level of *comfort*, which is progress but not the ultimate goal. Finally, the pinnacle of learning is reached: *reflex action*. The content has now become so much a part of us that it's instinctively applied—it has become a skill.

Moving the learner all the way from *aware* to *reflex action* requires time and repetition. This is where training usually fails—because of no follow-through—and often comes from the "Flavor of the Month" mentality organizations possess. Bringing in one program after another without following through not only prevents repetition, it creates cynicism in people. *Oh, great. Here we go again!* becomes their response to the next training venture. We can defeat cynicism, help people grow, and have a positive impact on our cultures by implementing an excellent training process—*and sticking with it*.

Ownership by Management: Though internal staff trainers are a valuable resource, in the end, it's the manager's job to train and develop people. In fact, it is their Number One obligation—every single day. Managers in outstanding organizations gain ownership of the training process by facilitating and teaching the training. Without ownership by managers, repetition will be nonexistent. Plus, managers might just send people off to training and when they come back, say, "I know that's what they taught you in the classroom, but that's not the way we do it here!" The lack of management support and follow-up is the fastest way to kill the effectiveness of training. Also, when managers are actively involved in the training process, they are better able to coach the content later on—and it sets the right example, too.

A training colleague of mine and a terrific presenter, Kevin Brown, was to speak at a hospital. The "sign-ups" for this voluntary program were light and when the CEO caught wind of it, he was not happy at all. "We're investing dollars and time, and people don't want to come?!" he exclaimed. So he sent out a broadcast email making the training mandatory, and every able person came—

except him. Exiting the auditorium, the HR director whispered to Kevin the understatement of the year: "There'll be some negative feedback on this."

Management, take ownership for training.

Consistent Message: The messages we send through training must be consistent over time and across all those trained. If Group #19 and Group #91 don't hear the same messages that Group #1 heard, confusion is the result, and confusion prevents action. Since this is the exact opposite of what training should do, the lack of consistency of message can be a big problem, especially for organizations that train hundreds or thousands of people. Make sure the training invested in conveys the same core messages over and over again for all to hear.

Easily Customized: Customization is important but highly misunderstood—and often a big waste of money. Customized training is not about having an organization's name embossed on the training tools, or having role-playing actors on DVD or the Web talking about specific products or services. It's all about *connection*—between the content and the problems.

Here's the formula for customizing training:

Problems + Practical Content + Conversation = Customization.

Connecting practical material to the problems, language, and culture of the organization, and giving learners ample time to explore it all through well-facilitated dialogue, results in wonderfully tailored training.

Support Tools: Every training program will have different types of tools, so the best comment I can make here is this: Less is more. Participants shouldn't be burdened with so many "take-aways" that the materials never get touched outside the classroom. If there's simply too much material or it is not practical, they'll wind up in the bottom drawer, lost among all those binders and piles of paper.

Specific Plan: Like anything that is done well, training needs to follow a plan. An effective training program lays out a road map to ensure that each step fits the culture, pace of work, and logistical issues of the organization—not to mention the people's developmental needs. Without a plan, the training becomes just a shot in the arm with little long-term impact.

These seven criteria for an effective training process are a great way to evaluate any training program. Lots of organizations espouse "People Are Our Greatest Asset," but only the outstanding ones support those words with training. In the view of Dennis Doran, president of Cambridge Medical Center, "We used to cut training when tight times came, but my dad was an educator, so he straightened me out on that. Ever since, I always make sure we keep training, no matter what. You have to keep developing people."

CHAPTER THIRTY-FIVE

Encourage One Another

When I work with a group, I'll often have them stand and stretch after an hour, since, as everybody knows, the mind can only absorb what the backside can handle. But I like to have people stretch with purpose, so I give them a quick exercise by instructing, "I want each of you to find three people, shake their hands, look them dead in the eye, and say, 'I appreciate you just the way you are!'" For a brief moment, there's an awkward silence, but then every group begins to engage. The laughter bubbles up, people loosen up, and it's a fun sixty seconds. It's not only fun, though—for some folks, the exercise has significance that goes well beyond their backsides.

One morning, I spoke to about sixty firefighters. Do you know any firemen? I live next to one. They are good people who see a lot of bad things. Typically they are helpful, smart, and courageous—but they can be a tough audience. When I am asked to do a training session with a crowd of firefighters, it's just, well—different. Adjectives like "emotive" and "touchy-feely" don't really come to mind. But I used my stand-and-stretch exercise anyway, and it went well. At the end of the workshop, a gray-haired guy of about fifty confided, "I've been awfully hard on my sixteen-year-old son lately, so I just called him and asked him to meet me at Denny's for lunch." He went on, "I need to tell him how much he means to me—and I won't even mention that he was still in bed when he answered his cell!"

On another occasion, a sales manager in Houston came to me shortly after a session and shared, "I just called my assistant. She works so hard and is so valuable to me and I haven't told her so in ages." And then there was the thirtysomething man with glistening eyes who said, "My wife and I separated three months ago. I never told her I appreciated her just the way she is. I hope it's not too late."

It's rarely too late to make that call, send that email, or mail that all-important note. Letting others know how much we appreciate them is simply an outstanding thing to do. And this is not about managing, coaching, or mentoring, though acts of encouragement certainly are a part of those realms, too. I'm talking about peer-to-peer encouragement and support. Colleague to colleague, each of us can say and do things that hearten others.

Having a culture in which people feel valued and appreciated is a big part of what makes an organization outstanding. Words of support between teammates go a long way toward making that culture a reality. In addition to the value it brings to the organization, it's meaningful for each of us as individuals, too. After all, what we sow, we reap.

Let's each see what we can do today to send a little encouragement another person's way.

CHAPTER THIRTY-SIX

Listen in All Directions

Bernie Marcus, one of the founders of Home Depot, who has served on several boards of directors for various organizations, said, "Whenever a new CEO is hired, we tell him or her, 'Don't do *anything* for the first three months other than shut your mouth, open your ears, and go around listening.'" That's spot-on counsel for any CEO, and listening is equally important for everyone in an organization, whether it's individuals listening to one another, the organization listening to its customers, or management listening to their people.

LISTENING TO ONE ANOTHER

I heard the term "multitasking" for the first time when on the phone with a client. As we talked, a loud *click-clacking* noise began to distract me, and soon became truly irritating. I finally asked, "Excuse me, what is that noise?" and she brightly replied, "Oh, I'm multitasking." *So that's what typing while someone is talking is called now,* I thought. *When I was young it was called rude.* It's also called not listening. It's like driving and talking on your cell phone. You can do either well, but not both. And chances are you'll get in an accident—or cause someone else to. I ended up having to repeat to her what I'd just said.

Yes, I admit, I "multitask," too. I imagine most everyone does, but that doesn't make it right—or wise. A mentor once said to me, "John, the mind can only hold one thought at a time." Because our minds move so quickly from one thing to another, it's easy to fool ourselves into believing that we really are doing many things well all at once. The reality is we do a disservice to others and ourselves when we try to concentrate on too much in one moment. In fact, I would suggest that when we do that there isn't much concentration going on at all. Let's put the distractions aside and really listen to one another.

LISTENING TO THE CUSTOMER

Kim Ramage, a district human resource manager at Best Buy and a twenty-year veteran of both the company and an ever-changing industry, says, "Our best employees are curious about the customer. They ask lots of questions so they can have rich dialogue and build relationships with people who visit our stores." Kim has it exactly right. Listening to the customer is all about being genuinely interested in what they need and what they want, and demonstrating this by reaching out to them with questions like, "How are we doing for you?" "What are your needs and wants?" "How can we be better?"

An organization that doesn't listen to its customers risks losing them. I asked a former regional trainer for a major restaurant chain how it was that the chain had just been swallowed up by what I perceived to be a smaller, lesser-known one. His response was a grim one: "That's what happens when you think you're right on menu items, pricing, and décor, and the guests are telling you otherwise—but you keep thinking you're right! It was like, 'What does the customer know?!'" He went on to explain that their same-store sales and profits had slipped and they'd become an easy takeover target, all because nobody was listening to the customer.

MANAGEMENT LISTENING TO THEIR PEOPLE

Here's an idea: Let's do a survey so all the employees can give their opinion, and then once we the organization have compiled the data, we'll do—*nothing*. I know that sounds cynical, but it happens every day. Or at least people have the *impression* that it does. I vividly recall a young man in his late twenties scribbling like mad—in pre-electronic days—all over a questionnaire that had been supplied by his company. Using a #2 pencil, he wrote furiously for an hour in the lunch room. It felt really, *really* good to express all his "concerns"—and be blunt!

It's been a long time since I've used a pencil for anything, but after I filled out that survey, I thought, *This is terrific! Things are gonna get better now!* Positive change was coming and I couldn't have been more excited! Four months later, I left the organization without ever hearing about the employee survey again. Did they learn anything of value from the information?

Did any changes come from it? What a waste. Whether you're a small business owner working with staff one-on-one or a large employer doing a formal survey, my advice is this: If you're not going to study the info gleaned and communicate the results back to people and then make some changes, then DO NOT ASK THE QUESTIONS!

Listening is something that's ultimately done by an individual. Yet an organization can also have a culture that encourages and supports listening in all directions and ways, and outstanding organizations do just that. As Mr. Marcus said, sometimes it's good to just "go around listening."

CHAPTER THIRTY-SEVEN

Coach, Moment to Moment

Coaching is one of the hottest topics in the organizational world. That's good, because coaching increases productivity, builds skills and trust, and creates loyalty. Coaching is essential to both the individual's and the organization's success. And it needn't be complicated. Too often we view coaching as a formal process where managers help people define objectives, encourage development, and review progress. All that may be important, but real coaching is about managers being engaged with their people—moment to moment.

The Miller family was dining at our favorite Applebee's restaurant, and our server was a trainee named Ben. It was Ben's second day on the job, and his shift supervisor, Darci, was at his side. Shortly after putting in our order, Ben and Darci arrived at our table with Ben carrying a big round tray loaded with various beverages destined for several customers. Holding the tray high in one hand, he carefully placed our drinks on our table. "Thanks," we said.

"You're welcome!"

And then the worst thing possible happened: In what seemed like slow motion, Ben's tray tilted and all the other drinks tumbled off, landing on the rug, an empty booth, and a few guests' shoes, including mine. One patron was even hit by a flying ice cube! Ben was clearly mortified, but Darci instantly reassured him, "Don't worry. It's okay. No problem." Meanwhile, an awkward silence had enveloped the room as customers tried not to stare and nobody knew quite what to say.

Just then we heard the terrible sound of breaking glass and shattering plates coming from the kitchen. Without skipping a beat, and with a smile on her face, Darci said to Ben, "See? *Everyone* does it!" The tension broke, customers laughed, and all was right with the world. Good coaching does that.

Our only son, Michael, worked as a teller at a Wells Fargo drive-thru bank during college. One day, an older man driving what was possibly an even older car, pulled into another teller's lane. His transaction was handled promptly, but before driving away, the gentleman suddenly pointed at Michael through the large plate glass window and angrily yelled, "Him! *Him* I don't like!" Mike, not recognizing the man at all—and totally caught off guard—clicked his microphone on and said, "Pardon me, sir?"

"*You*, I don't like *you*!" the man hollered again.

Sitting just out of sight was Mike's boss, Jennifer Infante. She knew that Mike has a quick wit and a dry sense of humor—and a mouth that can run ahead of his brain. (Wonder where he gets that?) It's a particular trait of Michael's that they'd talked about before, and now, seeing the situation unfold, Jen saw that a "teachable moment" was developing. Anticipating that Mike might be about to say something he shouldn't, she whispered, just loud enough for him to hear, "Mike, relax. Remember, he's a customer. Let it go." So Mike checked himself, smiled through the glass, and said, "Have a nice day, sir!" and watched the man drive off. Service disaster averted, thanks to a good boss doing her Number One job: coaching.

One cannot coach what one does not observe. Both of these stories demonstrate solid, in-the-moment coaching skills, but perhaps most important, they demonstrate that the supervisor was *there* when he or she needed to be. Most managers can't be by the side of every employee every minute of the day—nor should they be. But it's also true that managers cannot coach unless they are present. The best coaching happens day to day and moment to moment. Managers, be there.

CHAPTER THIRTY-EIGHT

Be Coachable

I met with Frank, an up-and-coming, thirtysomething vice president of a financial institution, the day after a leadership training project I had conducted with his senior staff. In our one-on-one, Frank asked for feedback on his management style and approach with his people. The salesperson in me was hoping to be of more help to Frank in the future (read: *Sell him something*), so I hesitated. But then I thought, *Well, he asked!* So I went for it.

I gave Frank the coaching he asked for, mentioning a few things he had said or done during the session that I felt could have been handled better. What I was really thinking—without saying it—was that Frank had ego problems. As far as I was concerned, the root cause of the things I'd seen was simply arrogance on his part. Well, that same arrogance worked against my hope of any future business with him. After he "listened" to my coaching, we shook hands, parted company, and I never saw or heard from Frank again. He had "shot the messenger." Not surprisingly, it appears that he ignored the advice. I heard later from others in his organization that he had changed nothing in his behavior.

I don't know if it's because I've been in the training industry for so long or if it's just that people see me as the neutral outsider, but clients often ask for feedback. "What do you see, John?" "How can we improve?" "What can we change?" And one thing I've learned is this: It is a rare day when people actually take coaching and do something with it—and how outstanding it is when they do.

My wife, Karen, and I decided to try a new church, just two miles from our home. After a few Sunday visits we liked it, and have been going there ever since. That's where I met Pastor Mark Hardacre: The Coachable One. Mark was an optometrist before feeling called into the ministry. At forty years old, he started on a new life path, which ultimately led him to being the pastor at our new church.

As Mark and I would shake hands and chat in the church foyer each week, we got to know each other.

One day, when Mark discovered that I am a "professional speaker," he asked me for a quick speaking tip. So I shared a thought, and he used it. Yes, you read that right. *He . . . used . . . it.* That was remarkable enough, but it isn't the end of the story. Mark is one who truly loves to learn—and improve. At first, we'd meet over breakfast and discuss the craft of speaking. Then he started emailing me his upcoming Sunday message, asking for input. I'd send it back with my comments, and on Sunday morning, I would sit in the early service, taking notes on the message *and* on Mark—the speaker. When the service ended, we'd both head to the foyer for a quick review. Mark would nod his head, jot a few notes, and then make the second service message even better.

Isn't that amazing? Think of the difference between these two men. Frank not only dismissed the feedback he had asked for, but shot the messenger, too. But Mark, instead of letting ego and arrogance get in his way, just keeps asking, "How can I improve what I do?" and "What can I do to grow?" And as he grows, his organization grows. Our new church is, by all measurements, succeeding. Exploding in size and outreach to the community, it's truly making a difference in people's lives. There are many reasons a church attracts people and achieves its goals, but I have no doubt that Mark's deep desire to learn and improve plays a major role.

Many speak of the need for continuous improvement. This important process can happen only when each of us makes a personal choice not only to be open to coaching, but to seek it out. For the good of the organization, and ourselves, let's be coachable.

CHAPTER THIRTY-NINE

Someone Needs to Be the Boss

Whenever a client asks someone from our team to speak, we first send them a questionnaire to help us gain some understanding of their culture, problems, and language. A question we always ask is: What are some complaints being voiced by people inside your organization? One client's response read like this: "People sometimes ask why upper management did this or that without getting their permission."

Permission?

When I was at Cornell University working toward my degree in business management, I just could not understand why I needed to take Astronomy 101 and English History. How in the world did those subjects relate to any of my academic or career goals? I fought it, complained about it, and probably would've failed them both if I hadn't finally realized that *I did not run the school!* If Cornell required them, then I needed to take them.

Then there's the professional ballplayer who became irate when word leaked out that his head coach was being let go. He threw a public tantrum and demanded to know why he hadn't been informed in advance. He apparently forgot that in spite of his fame, fortune, and immense God-given talent, he was still an employee of the organization, and they don't have to tell him anything they don't want to.

In the best-functioning organizations, people understand and respect the boundaries of their authority. They don't act like they're the boss if they're not, nor do they try to *avoid* acting like the boss if they are.

While I was facilitating a senior manager team session, the conversation moved into the serious arena of results, numbers, and profitability, and the CEO said about the oddest thing I've heard in my career. Regarding profit, he declared, "Hey, I don't want that ball!" I wondered if I'd heard him right. *Does this CEO not want to be accountable for the organization's profit?* Not surprisingly, it wasn't long after that meeting that the board of directors realized they didn't have the best person in the job.

I read an article somewhere that trumpeted the

"coming death of the CEO position" and the "rise of the team." Well, it might be a cool-sounding idea, but it doesn't wash with me. Teams, teamwork, and consensus-building are tools, not forms of governance. The bottom line is, the buck has to stop somewhere, and every division, district, department, and team within the organization needs to have clear lines of authority. When the building's on fire, we don't ask for input—someone needs to take charge! More broadly, decisions need to be made and someone has to be responsible for the success or failure of the team.

In spite of all the change we've seen over the years in management practices, and the new and different skills managers need to relate effectively to today's workforce, one thing hasn't changed: Someone still has to be the boss.

CHAPTER FORTY

Seek No Culprits

I arrived at a well-known chain hotel on a Monday to check in. The immediate look of confusion on the registration person's face was concerning. He then informed me that they had no reservation for me—and they were all booked up. "That can't be right," I said. "I just called on Saturday to confirm my reservation." His first question was, "Who did you talk to, sir?" I said, "I have no clue." He continued to search for my reservation and twice more asked me who I had spoken to. *I DON'T KNOW!!!* Finally, I asked for the manager. When he came out, I quickly explained the problem again, and he automatically asked—you guessed it—"Who did you talk to, sir?" Disbelieving, I said, "Why do you all insist on knowing who I spoke to?" He responded, "So we can talk to them about doing it right next time."

Wrong answer, wrong focus, and wrong for any organization's culture. Teaching and coaching is one thing, but looking for culprits is another. An executive I called on expressed a similar mind-set when she said, "John, we actually like to find the person who made the mistake, because if we don't do that, we believe individuals will hide behind systems and processes."

Nope. I don't buy it. Indicting people is never the best way to go.

I was working with a senior management team that had discovered several problems with its manufacturing process. When they learned that fully half of the supervisors had known of the problems for *five years*, the first question was, "Why didn't our managers tell us about these problems?!" rather than asking, "What have we done to create an environment where people are reluctant to speak up?"

What really struck me was that their approach was simply not going to solve the problem—or any problem, for that matter. In fact, it was this experience of people asking the wrong questions and demonstrating a lack of personal accountability that was a driving force behind writing the *QBQ!* book. I just couldn't stop wondering how this sort of thinking advances the ball, creates a solution, or wins people over. Of course, the answer is that it doesn't.

In an outstanding organization, when problems come to light, managers look to the culture that envelops people, and look hard at themselves before they begin searching for the culprit. They know that blame, finger-pointing, and scapegoating are not the way to go. Addressing problems with a "whodunit?" approach is a dangerous trap for any organization. Here are just a few reasons why a Culture of Culprit Catching hurts us:

IT'S A WASTE OF TIME AND ENERGY

A problem is almost never about one person. Yes, someone committed an error, but why? What made them think it was the correct thing to do? How were they trained? What else was going on at the time? The truth is, when the onion is peeled and a human error is really examined, it's almost never about what one individual did in one moment, but more about the organization's systems, processes, and environment. So, looking for a culprit is simply looking in the wrong place. It represents flawed thinking, and almost never leads to a real solution.

IT KEEPS US STUCK IN THE PAST

All problems are in the past, but solutions are right now. It's hardly possible to find a solution while we're pointing fingers at other people, in part because we're stuck in the past. Whatever happened happened. It's over and done. Focusing on finding solutions rather than finding scapegoats brings us into the present. The mantra inside an outstanding organization is often as simple as *Onward!* People there know it's better to keep moving forward.

IT CREATES A FEARFUL WORK ENVIRONMENT

Fear stifles creativity, desire, and motivation—along with virtually every other trait critical to being a stellar organization. A "heads will roll" mentality scares people, and why wouldn't it? Let's be honest: Fear is demoralizing. Which reminds me of a favorite saying:

The firings will continue until morale improves! Let's work each day to drive fear from the workplace.

IT DAMAGES RELATIONSHIPS

Trying to find out who needs to be lectured about "doing it right the next time" certainly won't create an environment that is conducive to healthy and productive relationships. People need to feel safe when reaching out to and relying on others. Only in an organizational culture that is fertile ground for trust, open communication, and mutual respect will these requirements for strong relationships grow.

When the Blame Game is in effect, people retreat and hunker down. Yes, we need to get to the root of a problem, but searching for culprits is the worst way to do it. Rather, let's focus our energy and invest our time in creating a climate where customers are served, problems are solved, and staff flourish. This is all best achieved by attacking problems, not people.

Chapter Forty-one

Skip the Vision Thing

For years gurus have been telling executives they need a vision for the organization. "Your people must catch the vision!" the experts have preached, while fad-oriented organizations forked over boatloads of cash, time, and energy to hear the message. You've seen it, I've seen it—but now I say, *Bunk!* There are at least four problems with the vision thing—and knowing them could save us a lot of, well, cash, time, and energy!

THE TERMS ARE RARELY DEFINED

In the Bible there's a story referred to as "The Tower of Babel." The short version is the people of the world, who are portrayed as all speaking a single language, decided to build a structure to reach to the Heavens with the purpose of supplanting God and glorifying humankind. Needless to say, God was none too pleased, so He shut down the effort by introducing new languages and confusing the tongues of the workers. Without common language, there was no communication or understanding—and the tower project failed.

Organizations can have the same problem when words are not clearly defined. Look at the popular terms tossed around: strategy, tactic, objective, target, guiding principle, core value, and . . . *mission* and *vision*. These last two are routinely offered up as interchangeable—but they're not. A vision is a picture on the screen of one's mind, so an organizational vision is what senior management hopes the entity will look and be like in the future. But the mission— which we explored in chapter three—is the crucial *why*. That is, it's the reason undergirding the entity's very existence. So, vision and mission are very different ideas. When we mix them up, not only is it confusing, but the organization misses the chance to get its far more critical *mission* into people's hearts and minds.

IT'S JUST AN EXERCISE

Many a senior team has worked feverishly to come up with "The Grand Vision," but sometimes the exercise seems to be little more than crossing an item off their *Management To-Do List*. Afterward, the new vision is hung on the wall where it's promptly forgotten. For one CEO, it wasn't even on a wall. When asked about the firm's vision by a visitor, he couldn't remember the words till he found them on a slightly crumpled piece of paper in the bottom drawer of his desk! Why bother to define a vision if you can't remember it—and likely don't mean it? Organizations get caught up in way too many activities they don't even believe in or care about just because a consultant, a new book, or their own training department told them they should do it.

IT'S NOT HELPFUL TO MOST PEOPLE

Candidly, the vision is simply not germane to what most people do each day. Knowing what executives see on the screen of their minds fails to help many people at any level perform their day-to-day job. It does not enhance productivity, increase revenue, lower costs, or help things get done fast. Also, some vision statements are simply meaningless slogans, like, "Be the Best," "Become a Great Place to Work," "Be the World Leader in Our Industry," and "Be First." Short and sweet, but not helpful at all.

IT'S ALL A MYTH ANYWAY

Question: Do you know anyone who can see tomorrow? If so, I want them to manage my investments! The assumption that senior managers should be able to see the future has become a true burden, and causes them to feel like failures because they cannot—and heaven forbid they admit that to anyone! The truth is, when people who supposedly had vision that resulted in success are asked to speak in hindsight, what comes to light is they were blessed with good intuition and instincts, a market that turned in their favor, a competitor who stumbled, or just plain good luck. I've talked to senior people who chuckled, saying, "Better lucky than good!" We simply cannot see the future, and constantly pressing executives to do so is as pointless as an interviewer asking a job applicant the overused, canned question, "Where do you see yourself in five years?" Honestly, what do we expect a candidate to say? If it were me, since I can't see the future, my answer would be, "God willing—*alive!*"

I'm not saying there's absolutely no value in the "visioning" process, but let's keep it in perspective. As one senior manager said, "I'm fine with three- to five-year plans and wordsmithing the vision, but I am *more* concerned with what my team gets done before lunch!" Truly, for most people in an outstanding organization, it's not so much about the future, but the present. And in this current moment, hopefully, each of us is focusing on our job, excelling in our work, and being the best we can be.

CHAPTER FORTY-TWO

Treat Vendors like People

Every single day organizations buy all kinds of stuff—from technology systems to cubicles to paper towels—because they need all kinds of stuff to succeed. I believe that the exceptional organizations treat the vendors that provide these wares like customers.

Let's say you have an outside sales rep calling on your organization—is she a customer of yours? You bet she is. Why? Because, as the 360-Degree Customer Concept says, she has legitimate expectations of you. Expectations such as being listened to, getting paid expeditiously, being treated respectfully, having phone calls and emails returned in a timely manner, and receiving thanks for a job well done. Communication and courtesy are things that people who sell to us want—and deserve.

In the 1950s, American statistician, professor, and

lecturer Dr. W. Edwards Deming helped Japanese industry rebuild itself after World War II. From that experience and others, he developed his now famous 14 Points of Management. In point #4, Deming said that organizations should build long-term relationships of loyalty and trust with suppliers. The reason to do so is this: It is good business. No organization can achieve its goals without their suppliers, and a positive, trusting relationship returns more value over time than one that's focused only on price and terms.

Do you see your vendors as partners—even colleagues—who help you succeed? Or, conversely, are interactions with them adversarial, filled with give-us-a-better-price friction and fill-out-these-vendor-docs-in-triplicate demands? How many hoops does your organization make a supplier jump through to be of service? Are your contracts and procurement policies so lopsided they favor only the buyer?

While hammering out a training agreement with the food company Schwan's, Kim Stephens, a director in their organizational development department, emailed me saying their legal department had "redlined" our document and he was returning it to me for my review. In our email dialogue, I asked a simple question and got back an outstanding answer:

John: "Tell me, is Schwan's saying no negotiating on the red-line comments that your lawyer made on the contract?"

Kim: "Not at all. If there's something you don't agree with, we'll talk about it. Marvin Schwan's spirit is still alive here. As he always desired, agreements need to be win-win for both parties."

Now that's an organization that knows how to treat the outsider.

Take it from a guy who has sold to organizations for many years: It is a real negative for the outsider when an organization makes the buy-sell process arduous and burdensome. On the other hand, when a customer treats a vendor with respect, the supplier's desire to serve increases many times over. And let's not forget: Even if someone is offering a product or service we *don't* want or need, they still should be told swiftly, in a candid and kind fashion.

Though it's easy to forget sometimes when we're on the procurement side of things, vendors deserve to be treated as any of us want to be: as good, hard-working people doing their best each day. Outstanding organizations understand, as did Dr. Deming, that treating vendors like people is not just the right thing to do, it's good for our organizations.

CHAPTER FORTY-THREE

Stay Alarmed

Do you recall the last time you were walking through a parking garage or a store lot and you heard a car alarm blaring away, penetrating your brain? They can be pretty irritating. In fact, the noise was so intrusive that you did—*nothing!* That's right, nothing. Why? Because we have heard so many errant car alarms screaming into the day and night, they've actually lost their purpose. We are no longer alarmed, as they've become part of the cacophony of noise that makes up our world. In the end, vehicle alarms have become mostly ineffective, and the real problem is we stop watching for the actual dangers the alarms were meant to warn us of in the first place.

One of the great risks to an organization is complacency. When things are going well, it's easy to start thinking we have it made, that we've got it all figured out. Success can be very seductive, because success affirms—in our minds—that what we're doing is right. It can prevent us from looking for better ways to do what we're doing. But thoughts like these should set off alarms in our head because, the truth is, advancement does not equal arrival, and we can only coast in one direction: downhill.

Irv Schuetzner spent thirty years with one of the most famous general merchandise retailers ever, a department store chain that had already existed a hundred years when I shopped them as a child. In his time there, Irv had a stint in the training department and the opportunity, along with his training colleagues, to go in front of senior management to talk about the need for more training at the store level. As he tells it, the training team shared their recommendation to the top group as the execs stared blankly throughout the presentation, showing little interest—and then the training proposal was roundly denied. Looking back, Irv is convinced that each senior manager in the boardroom that day was so out of touch with reality at the store level, they actually thought everything was just fine. Today that organization is on a not-so-esteemed list titled:

"Memorable Companies That Have Vanished For-ever." I guess they didn't hear the alarms.

On the flip side, I sat down with Michael, the CEO of an agricultural retail supply chain, a Harvard graduate, and son of the founder. They were having a terrific year as market share was up, along with earnings and profit. They were even buying store facilities from their competitors. Yet even with all that, Michael told me one of their guiding principles was this: Be open to the 1% possibility. "We must never get to the point where we think we know it all," he explained with a smile. "So we constantly keep in mind there's at least a one percent possibility that we can do things better." And consider this observation from Steve Szilagyi, senior vice president of distribution at Lowe's Home Improvement: "One thing I've found to be true here is there is a restless and relentless desire to improve everything we do." Perfectly said. I bet Irv from the vanished chain would like to have seen some of that kind of thinking!

Complacency is a state of satisfaction combined with an unawareness of potential danger, and it's often characterized by one word: smug. Outstanding organizations know that "smug" doesn't work. They understand the need to beat back complacency again and again and again so that they, too, won't vanish. To do that, they talk about "continuous improvement" and "process enhancement," but the goal can be stated this way, too: We must remain vigilant and open to the 1 percent possibility.

However we say it, the message is the same: Stay alarmed.

CHAPTER FORTY-FOUR

Tend to the Little Things

Miller Child Number Six, Jazzy Joy, has an uncanny habit that, at times, has driven us nuts: She states the obvious. It all started when she was a toddler. "Dad, it's Saturday." "Mom, it's seven o' clock." "Dad, the sun is shining." "Mom, Bear is a girl dog." It's as if she took on the role of roaming our home proclaiming what she believes is news. So we nicknamed her the "Town Crier." The only thing missing was, "Hear ye! Hear ye!" Now that she's a teen and doesn't do it as much, we all think of it as cute.

But, honestly, sometimes the obvious needs to be said. So at the risk of making you crazy, too, I want to state what should be incredibly clear to all organizations: It's really important to take care of the little things.

I regularly stop at the Conoco Gas N' Go on

Bridge Street in my town of Brighton, Colorado. Their gas is no cheaper than the others and it is four blocks out of my way. But I still go there—regularly. Of course, now you want to know why, right? Well, it's simple: clean restrooms.

The owner, Don, provides his customers with the cleanest, shiniest, and possibly most germ-free bathrooms west of the Mississippi. He doesn't sell other things I tend to buy such as coffee, mints, and my favorite daily newspaper. But the station that's closer—and does sell those things—has restrooms so dirty I wouldn't take my dog in there. Maybe they think a clean bathroom is an unimportant detail. I don't know, but Don understands otherwise. And the lesson he offers for outstanding organizations of all sizes is that when it comes to taking care of the customer, there are no little things. Everything matters. Everything makes an impression. Every single thing we do will make our customers more—or less—loyal.

I'm sure I'll keep going back to Don for as long as he's there. I appreciate the attention he pays to what's obvious to him but not to others.

Tend to the little things—today.

CHAPTER FORTY-FIVE

Put Performance Before Titles

I asked a new client how many managers they had. She came back with this question: "Now, are you talking about those who actually manage other people or those that just have the 'manager' title?"

Huh?

Have you seen "title inflation"? It's quite common in some industries. A person can be a lone contributor who manages no one but themselves, but they're still an AVPIS—Assistant Vice President of Important Stuff! And it's not just about the titles bestowed, but how people *with* certain titles are treated by their organization, like when given premium, close-to-the-front-door parking spots, for example. Corporations and their CEOs, churches and their head pastors, academia and their presidents, school districts and their superintendents, and nonprofits and their directors are all guilty of this. Don't get me wrong. Having an important-sounding title is not inherently a bad thing, of course. But in truly outstanding organizations, it's not titles that matter, but how well we perform and serve.

I arrived at the Cleveland airport for my evening flight with dread in my heart. I needed to get to Portland, Oregon, that night, and I was taking the last flight west—something one who *has* to be somewhere on time never wants to do. On top of that, I had to connect through the incredibly busy, always chaotic O'Hare International Airport.

We pulled away from the gate on time, but then a "ground hold" due to congestion in Chicago caused us to sit on the runway. Going nowhere fast, my worry meter kicked in. Meanwhile, I was fortunate enough to be sitting next to a United Airlines pilot— Captain Terry Callaghan—who was catching a ride to O'Hare to pilot a flight to Germany. As you may know, airline pilots operate in a hierarchical, seniority-based system, and only the most senior pilots fly the foreign routes. Add that to the captain's hat in his lap and his distinguished gray hair, and I knew he was an experienced professional. Chatting with him, he was able to explain the reasons behind the delay, which helped a little, but I still really needed to be in Portland that night—and we were losing precious minutes fast!

We finally took off. I figured that if we landed at 7:15 P.M., I could still make my 7:45 flight west. (I can sprint through an airport as fast as anyone.) We did land at 7:15, but then we began a seemingly endless taxi to the gate. Captain Terry, seeing my concern, asked me a good question: "Did you check your luggage through or give it up at plane side?"

"Plane side," I answered despondently. We both knew I was at the mercy of how fast the baggage handlers brought the bags up to the jetway. It was now 7:30 and . . . Captain Terry to the rescue! "You know, John, I could wait for your bag while you dash to your flight," he said. "When it comes up, I'll bring it down to your gate. If I don't make it in time, I'll get it on the first morning flight to Portland for you."

"Uh, really? You'd do that?" I asked. He said he would and I started to believe—especially since we'd now arrived at the gate. But then the flight attendants wouldn't let us off due to a six-inch gap between the jetway bridge and the plane door. So there we all stood, staring at a half-foot gap that might as well have been a half mile wide.

Finally, we were released at 7:34. I had eleven minutes. Terry slapped me on the back and said, "You can do it, John!" I ran. I made it. *Whew!*

Minutes later, sitting in my new seat, I noticed a flight attendant pointing at me. Then I saw Captain Terry Callaghan himself—with his very impressive captain's hat now perched atop his head and an ear-to-ear smile—strutting down the aisle to deliver my bag to me! I could tell from the faces of other passengers that I wasn't the only one to notice, and I was now certain that everyone was murmuring, "Who is this passenger who gets his luggage personally delivered by a captain? Is he a celebrity?" So I let them all think I'm famous, though, of course, I'm not. I'm just a guy who was blessed to sit next to a man willing to put performance and service above title and position.

Captain Terry has reached the pinnacle of his profession. He is used to being completely in charge. In his world, the captain could be called The Supreme Commander, The Head Honcho, or The Big Cheese. Simply put, he is the final authority—on everything. People in positions like these often exude self-importance, bordering on arrogance. They might even demand the best parking space, along with a personalized sign.

But that's not Captain Terry. He is an excellent role model for people at any level in any organization. Though his title carries significant weight and responsibility, he is focused on serving people. In fact, Captain Terry is such a special guy, I bet he parks in the economy lot and catches the shuttle like the rest of us. Quite honestly, in outstanding organizations, you find a lot of people just like him.

CHAPTER FORTY-SIX

Don't Stagnate: Turnover Can Be a Good Thing

The Dead Sea is "dead" because there's no turnover. The Jordan River flows in, but nothing flows out. It is in a permanent state of stagnation.

Stagnate: To stop developing, growing, progressing, or advancing; to be or become sluggish and dull; to be or become stale or foul from standing, as a pool of water.

Why do I mention this? Because too many have bought into the myth that turnover is bad for an organization.

Chatting with Dennis, the founding pastor of a large church, he declared with a smile, "John, in twenty-one years we've only let two people go!" I can understand why he'd be proud of that—too much turnover can certainly be a problem—but outstanding organizations realize that stagnation can be an even bigger problem. When Dennis made that comment, a client from way back popped quickly into my mind. Dan White, a VP of sales with a medical device firm, told me that his father had spent his whole career in sales and sales management, and that he loved calling his dad to share what was going on "in the trenches." During one friendly father-and-son sales chat, Dan boasted that he hadn't lost a salesperson in two years. After a pause, his father replied, "Well, son, then you and your management team are doing something wrong."

The truth is, any strength taken to an extreme becomes a weakness. Too much turnover is a bad thing, of course, but too little turnover can be a problem, too. Candidly, organizations too often hold on to people who aren't performing—or are underperforming. The reasons behind this management mistake are several: wanting to avoid the cost of bringing on a new person, fearing the potential impact on morale of letting a longtime employee go, and untrained managers failing to coach, counsel, and confront effectively, thus allowing personnel problems to persist. Whatever the reason, the truth remains—sometimes we have to weed the garden. I'm not saying go out and terminate someone today just to create turnover, but we must not forget the significant worth new people and fresh ideas bring to an organization.

Let's not allow our organizations, departments, and teams to stagnate. Keep turnover in perspective—it can be a good thing.

CHAPTER FORTY-SEVEN

Try! Risk! Grow!

Tasha, our youngest, loves the sport of gymnastics—and she's darn good. She has both a natural ability and a strong desire. So I built her a balance beam that sits about two inches off the ground. Why so low? Well, so she wouldn't get hurt when she falls—*and I want her to fall*. I want her to try new things and stretch herself so she can be as good as she wants to be. The reality is, with the balance beam, you can't excel without falling off . . . a lot. Imagine how many times an Olympic gymnast who wins the gold must have fallen off the beam in her lifetime. Falling is part of the process of learning and improving. So it's not that I really want Tasha to fall—I want her to be *willing* to fall. I want her to embrace the risk and keep trying and trying and trying some more, because that's what it takes to be the best.

A sports psychologist would say that those who win on the beam think differently from those who don't. The high achievers approach the apparatus saying to themselves, "Falling off is good. Let's do some of that today!" If Tasha approaches the balance beam thinking, *I mustn't fall off,* chances are she'll never get on in the first place. Or if she does get on, she'll play it too safe to become a champion.

Many people view life cautiously—as something from which they must not fall—and if they work for an organization that supports their natural reticence with a culture that discourages risk-taking, there are costs. One middle manager told me, despondently, "Sometimes people try to stand up and do something new and different, and they immediately get slapped right back to where they came from. Not much changes around here." That's the real danger for any organization that doesn't promote risk-taking: Nothing changes.

In outstanding organizations, people try things they've never tried before. They take actions that are uncomfortable. They engage in behaviors that might bring the pain of failing—and they do so in an environment that supports their efforts. The organization encourages risk and allows failure. "Try!" "Risk!" "Grow!" is the message. "Climb on that beam, and if you fall off, we'll praise you for the risk you took, the mistakes you made, and the lessons learned—and then have you do it all over again."

Be Outstanding

A rehab patient suffering from the effects of a stroke, who might've been considered a "difficult" patient by most standards—poor mobility, low endurance, and little strength—checked into Ashley Regional Medical Center. But Ashley Regional is no run-of-the-mill place when it comes to patient care. They quickly encouraged her to get out of bed and into a chair, and to eat on her own. They found volunteers to do crafts with her, and helped her to regain the use of her hands. On holidays, the staff decorated her room in bright colors, and brought extra clothing or a hairdryer and curling iron from home. In short, they love their work and care about people—and the patient's recovery was remarkable.

A car owner noticed fluid beneath her vehicle and called All American Quick Lube at 6:20 P.M. The friendly voice at the other end of the phone line said to come over, even though the shop had closed already. When she arrived, they found a cracked engine hose and called their parts supplier. The supplier had the part in stock, but it was too late to deliver. Meanwhile, as all this was happening, the customer realized she'd forgotten her purse! When she confessed her oversight, the response was, "Don't worry about that, let's get you all fixed up!" and she was handed $20 along with the keys to one of their own cars and told, "Go pick up the part while we get your car ready for repair. You can pay us tomorrow."

A guest at a Hilton hotel forgot his cell phone charger and went to the front desk for help. He and the staff searched the hotel's "lost and found" bin of chargers, but none fit his phone. They saw the customer's frustration and told him to leave his phone with them. Later that day, he learned that they'd gone to the hotel basement, dug through another box of chargers, found one that worked, and charged the guest's cell to the max. When he offered a tip, it was declined. They said that it was "their pleasure."

Now, the truth is, in each of these stories it wasn't "they" who did any of this. It was an individual. At the medical center it was a nurse named Dawn; at the Quick Lube it was the owner, Jason; and at the Hilton it was a woman named Angela. It's not "they" with whom customers, employees, vendors, donors, and volunteers interact—*it's people*. But even though we all see organizations through the people representing them, it's still the *organization* that ultimately gets the credit—or the blame. The message is this: If we want an outstanding organization then each of us must personally *be* outstanding.

I've mentioned the principle of personal account-ability at various times throughout this book, but the fact is that personal accountability underlies the whole concept of the outstanding organization. It's through individuals practicing accountability that the 47 beliefs, principles, and actions we've discussed come to life. Think of the people we've met in these pages: Michelle at Husqvarna, who delivered the product late on a Friday; Bill, the school superintend-ent who sets the perfect tone with his team; Jim, my boss from days gone by who was an outstanding manager; Dennis, the head of Cambridge Medical Center who believes in training and keeps it in the budget even in tough times; Gayle at Head Start who owned an important decision; and the unnamed Air France pilot who declared to all the customers, "No excuses!" Rather than complaining, procrastinating, and blaming, each of these people asked, "How can *I* make my organization outstanding?" That's personal accountability in action, and no organization can be its best without it.

This brings us to you. You're someone who cares about "improving the place" or you wouldn't have read this book. I also bet you want to be part of an outstanding organization, since no one gets out of bed in the morning thinking, *I want to work for a mediocre company today!* We all love to be involved with first-rate, thriving organizations, but wanting to be part of one and actively contributing toward making our organization outstanding are very different things. Since you must be in the latter crowd, and are ready and excited to get to work, the question is, what's next?

I recommend, since repetition is the motor of learning, that you reread and reexplore *Outstanding!*—but not necessarily front to back. First, revisit the Table of Contents and look for your favorite "way," or the one that's critical to your organization right now. Next, go to that chapter and study it again. Finally, call yourself to action with questions like:

What specific action will I take to apply this idea?

When will I do it?

Who will I ask to follow up with me to ensure I have done it?

Once you've done this for one chapter, repeat the process and choose another idea to put into action. Do this again and again until you've worked your way through the entire book. You can work on it as often as you like, but I'd recommend no more than a week or two lag time between chapters. Consider this exercise to be an ongoing process of learning *and* application.

Also, remember that one key to learning is timing. Thus, different ideas in *Outstanding!* will be more important and relevant at different times. So even if you feel one of the ideas here doesn't apply today, don't let that keep you from considering it at a later date. You should be able to keep going through the book back and forth—and back again.

Whatever you do, please do *not* put *Outstanding!* on a shelf to collect dust. Keep it handy on your desk, in your car, or at home so it can serve as what it's meant to be: a guide, a road map, and a handbook to be used over time to help your organization fulfill its potential.

I said in the introduction that I wrote this book because I believe people fire organizations—but they don't fire the outstanding ones. By taking our 47 "ways to make your organization exceptional" to heart and putting them to work, you can help your organization be one of those great ones—one that people want to buy from, sell to, invest in, volunteer at, and work for. And one that never gets fired. On top of that, not only will your *organization* become outstanding, but *you* will stand out, too.

I wish you the best in all your efforts.

Be outstanding!

The Story Behind the Story

It was 1976, disco was hot, and I was eighteen. Still residing in my boyhood town of Ithaca, New York, I asked the cutest sixteen-year-old girl I'd ever seen if she would go to a movie with me. When Karen said yes, the journey began.

Since nobody can see the future, we surely didn't know what was on life's horizon for us. After I earned my Cornell University diploma and Karen her registered nursing degree, we married on the first day of summer 1980 and moved west. The Big Corporation had offered me a job and we were on our way!

Over the next six years, we lived in Minnesota, Montana, Missouri, and then Minnesota again. It was there that I saw a "Help Wanted" ad seeking a "high-energy, successful salesperson" to sell management and sales training programs to Minneapolis/ St. Paul organizations. Truthfully, I'd never sold before, but I knew I was high energy! Within a month I left my corporate job, joined the small training firm that ran the ad, and started calling on and selling to the corporate world. My prospects were sales managers, VPs, CEOs, plant GMs, and branch managers in public and private companies—and never have I had so much fun! Neither did I see what was coming: Many wonderful years of selling, facilitating, consulting, speaking, writing—and learning.

Lots of learning.

You see, while *Outstanding!* is the outcome of my experiences, that's not the whole story. In reality, *Outstanding!* would not have come to be without some very special people in my life.

My wife, Karen, who encouraged me to answer that newspaper ad and then said, "Go ahead and take the job, make the career change. We'll be OK"— and has stood with me ever since.

My dad—the pastor and Ivy League wrestling coach—who was a powerful influence, teaching me many things. *Thanks, Pop!*

The clients—the many, many clients since 1986— who taught me, probably without really knowing they were doing any teaching at all. They had so much to say I wish I could thank each of them.

All seven outstanding Miller children. And especially Tara, who helped me come up with the title

Outstanding! and our oldest, Kristin, who now works with her dad traveling the country, speaking, teaching, and training. Her input on the manuscript was invaluable.

John Duff, my favorite editor and publisher, who provided a calm hand and voice throughout the chaotic writing process.

My older brother "EJ" who asks me "So how's business?" absolutely every single time we talk.

And finally, David Levin, author of *Don't Just Talk, Be Heard!* David came alongside me in the 1990s to be my speaking coach, friend, cheerleader—and co-author of every book I've ever written, including this one. I wouldn't have gotten here without him.

To each of you I say not only thanks, but also this: *You* are outstanding!

John G. Miller
Denver, Colorado, USA
John@OutstandingOrganization.com

To EXPLORE *how you can bring* **Outstanding!** *to your organization, visit us at:*

www.OutstandingOrganization.com

To LEARN ABOUT
"Personal Accountability and the QBQ!"
stop by this site:

www.QBQ.com

Helping businesses, organizations, and families make personal accountability a core value.

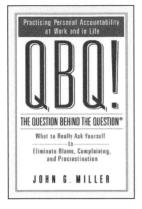

QBQ!	**Flipping the Switch**	**Outstanding!**
ISBN 978-0-399-15233-7	ISBN 978-0-399-15295-5	ISBN 978-0-399-15640-3